LIVE *Last*

MARK 9:35

KEITH NEWMAN

dustjacket

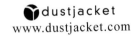

dustjacket
www.dustjacket.com

DEDICATION

Dedicated to my mom, whose legacy lives on.
Through words and deeds she taught
me what it means to live last.

———————— ● ————————

CONTENTS

FOREWORD

I've discovered that some people can live by a certain principle but not reflect on it and describe it to others. Other people can enthusiastically communicate something, but tragically there is no evidence they're living it. In Live*Last* Keith Newman shares a great truth that he also lives out.

Keith has a way of warmly welcoming every person he meets. And the more you get to know him the more you like him. Maybe it's the stories he tells or his sense of humor. Or is it perhaps his transparency and humility? While all those things are true of him, there's something deeper and more comprehensive.

It took me a while to put my finger on it, and finally he gave me the clue. It's his Live*Last* life. I'm so glad he's written about it. Live*Last* powerfully points to the words of Jesus in Mark 9:35— *Whoever wants to be first must take last place and be the servant of everyone else* (NLT).

Live*Last* is powerful because of its source. Jesus taught it as the very foundation of His disciple-making movement, which would go on to change the world. Live*Last* is transformative because of its strength. It is a tangible act of humility that invites God to be for us and not against us.

One of my mentors was a lay leader in our church who later served as CEO of a multinational company. The most memorable counsel I received from Bob was "Sit in the 'power seat' lightly. There was someone occupying it before you, and there will be someone in it following you. You don't own it–you only keep it warm for a while." As I learned to practice his advice, it transformed me personally and caused me to lead differently. It brought new freedom and paved the way for subsequent succession to the fruitful leadership of others.

Someone asked me recently, "What is the most powerful leadership lesson you've ever learned?" It is certainly this— "God opposes the proud but gives grace to the humble" (James 4:6 NLT). Live*Last* is the practical expression of humility that creates an inflow of God's grace. Keith not only lives it, but in Live*Last* he describes it in a way that we can all learn. That learning will bring a transformation and freedom as we follow in the footsteps of Jesus.

Wayne Schmidt
General Superintendent, The Wesleyan Church
Fishers, Indiana

INTRODUCTION

What if your dreams don't come true?

What if you fail?

Happy questions, right? Exactly the kinds of questions that make you want to keep reading—well, maybe not? Unachieved dreams and disappointing hopes need few reminders, but I hope you will persevere—because I believe you will find yourself in good company. Every single one of us has dreams that don't come true and stories sprinkled with failure. Some of us simply hide it better than others.

So what if your dreams
don't come true? What if you fail?

I begin with a bit of a confession that may damage my credibility with some of you. At our house we don't watch a lot of television, but when we do, we watch Hallmark movies. Will anyone else admit to viewing these works of art? In my defense, I watch them somewhat reluctantly. My wife watches them, and when I'm in the room with her when one is showing, I generally multi-task and make fun of it. You see, I have this gift of determining in the first ten minutes of the movie exactly what's going to happen. I know who the good guys are, who the bad guys are, and who's going to end up with whom in the end. Now it's not that I have the gift of prophecy, because I don't—it's just that Hallmark movies are so formulaic and so predictable that if you've seen one, you might as well have seen them all! Spoiler alert: One hour and forty minutes into every Hallmark movie there will be some major conflict (AKA drama), and the two people who are supposed to end up together look as if they're going different directions. But then, miraculously, one hour and fifty minutes into every Hallmark movie, through something less than divine intervention, the conflict is resolved and the two end up back together to live happily ever after—or so it goes.

Be assured of the following message that can be confirmed by anyone who is the least bit self-aware:

Your life will not be as predictable as a Hallmark movie!

What I can guarantee is that you will have conflict and it may not wait until the one-hour-and-forty-minute mark. While we hope and pray that you will live happily ever after, life is not like a Hollywood script, especially a Hallmark one.

Great books, great movies, and great stories all share one thing in common in my opinion: they contain many moments that could be described as *cliffhangers*.

Cliffhangers appeal to our curiosity. In these moments you truly don't know which way the story is going to go. Used effectively, they keep us turning pages in a novel or tuning in again next week. When I was a kid I watched the original version of the television show *Batman*—perhaps one of the poorest acted and scripted television shows of all time (my apologies to Adam West, Burt Ward, and Alan Napier). At the end of many episodes there would be a cliffhanger and the announcer would come on and say, "Will Batman get there in time to save Robin? Join us next week, same Bat time, same Bat channel!" And we did!

In a quality cliffhanger, someone is hanging on for dear life and things could turn out great or could be disastrous. There are opportunities for heroism, chances to be snatched from the jaws of victory, and vice versa.

No pressure here, but what I'm talking about is this: What will the rest of your life be like? You don't know. You have hopes, dreams, even great expectations—but you don't know. Your life is a bit of a cliffhanger!

One of my very favorite C. S. Lewis quotes seems appropriate here:

> *You can't go back and change the beginning,*
> *but you can start where you are*
> *and change the ending.*

The possibilities for your future and for all those whose lives you intersect are enormous, but it begins with a simple yet profound decision. Let me tell you in advance that most people do not choose this path, for if they did, our world would be a much better place, a much kinder place, and certainly a much happier place.

What's the decision? For that you'll need to keep reading.

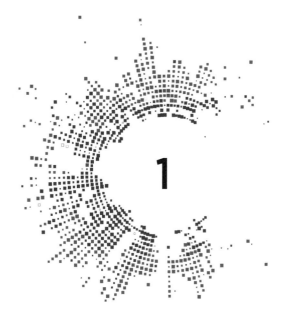

Live*Last*

What do you want, really want out of life?

A true leader has the confidence to stand alone, the courage to make tough decisions and the compassion to listen to the needs of others. He does not set out to be a leader but becomes one by the equality of his actions and the integrity of his intent.
—Douglas MacArthur

*B*ut I'm not a leader. If you make any decisions at all, then I believe you *are* a leader. Leadership is ultimately, in my opinion, all about stewardship. What are we doing with what we've been given? Not what we hope to have, dream about

1

having, what we want or are even working to get—what are we doing with what we've been given? How do we take an inventory and then begin to maximize however much or little is at our disposal? So, with stewardship as an important component of leadership, that makes everyone breathing and everyone reading this book a leader. I love thinking about leadership, talking about leadership, reading about leadership, writing about leadership, and praying about leadership. I especially love looking to the example of Jesus and learning what He taught about leadership while on earth. While He never invited anyone to come hear Him lecture on leadership or announced a class on leadership or conducted a forum on leadership, what He did do was call a group of guys to join Him on a journey, and they had a three-and-a-half-year unaccredited, very intentional educational experience.

The disciples may have been some of the slowest learners around. Often I feel as if I'm in that same group. Notice these words from the Gospel of Mark:

*And they came to Capernaum. And when he was in the house he asked them, "What were you discussing on the way?" But they kept silent, for on the way they had argued with one another about who was the greatest. And he sat down and called the twelve. And he said to them, **"If anyone would be first, he must be last of all and servant of all."** And he took a child and put him in the midst of them, and taking him in his arms, he said to them, "Whoever receives one such child in my name receives me, and whoever receives me, receives not me but him who sent me"* (Mark 9:33–37).

Imagine how uncomfortable it must have been when Jesus asked the question, "What were you discussing on the way?" They knew. He knew. I'm not sure they knew that He knew. Every time I speak, but especially when I have the privilege of speaking to college students, I try to use at least one show-and-tell moment. Jesus was the very best at show-and-tell!

Jesus called the disciples together, sat down (don't miss the significance of His posture), and then gave them instruction and illustrated by placing a child in the center of their circle.

Here is His core message, and it's one that's countercultural, completely backward to what is most common:

If anyone would be first,
he must be last of all and servant of all.

I describe this idea with two words: *live last!*

I'm on a bit of a mission to create and encourage Live*Lasters*, people who will look around the room or right in front of them and choose the least attractive assignment, the job that no one else seems to want to do.

One of the biggest decisions that any of us makes is determining what we're going to do with our lives. It's been my experience that the happiest and most fulfilled people are Live*Lasters*, people who determine that they're going to serve often and serve well. They choose the end of the line, the second mile, the place where you will seldom find a crowd. Movies are seldom made about Live*Lasters* and their life stories often don't make it into a book, but the impact of their investment in the lives of others creates a legacy recorded in heaven and a blessing on earth.

The decision to be a Live*Laster* is open to everyone who has ever walked this planet. If you're awake, then you're eligible. There are no height, weight, or IQ requirements. There's no waiting or wondering whether or not your service is needed. It is voluntary and there are immediate openings. The benefits are internal, external, and eternal. For most, being a Live*Laster* will not come naturally. It is a willful decision with a wonderful outcome.

Though slow to learn and maybe even slower to embrace, the disciples of Jesus finally bought into the message, and their lives of service continue to impact the world today. Choosing to be last, or least, or weak is countercultural today, but the reality is that it was going against the flow in the first century too. So how do we handle the disappointments of flops, failures, or fumbles? We follow in the footsteps of Jesus and choose to live last.

Near the end of His life on earth, Jesus had another show-and-tell moment with His disciples. Scripture tells us in John 13:4–5:

> *He got up from the meal, took off his outer clothing, and wrapped a towel around his waist. After that, he poured water into a basin and began to wash his disciples' feet, drying them with the towel that was wrapped around him.*

This scene from Scripture is commonly known as the Last Supper, and we know that there came a moment when Jesus did what no one else in the room thought of doing—or if they had thought about it, they decided that they did not want to do it. Jesus "wrapped a towel" around His waist, which means He took an apron commonly worn by slaves, tied around them when at work to keep their clothes clean, and He washed dusty, dirty, probably smelly feet. With humility, the King of Kings and Lord of Lords took the posture and position of a slave and demonstrated what it means to live last. I have to believe that it was a mental picture that was seared into the lives of the disciples; something they could never forget.

What about us? Do we look for ways to serve, to do what no one else wants to do, or are we seeking a status and strata that allows us to enjoy the benefits of others serving us? I hear the echo of a good word from thousands of years ago:

As for me and my household, we will serve the Lord.
(Joshua 24:15)

Choosing service was a great decision then and a powerful one now.

Questions for Reflection

1. Who has been a Live*Laster* model for your life?

2. What are the characteristics you have seen in your favorite Live*Laster*?

3. How could you be more intentional in your service today?

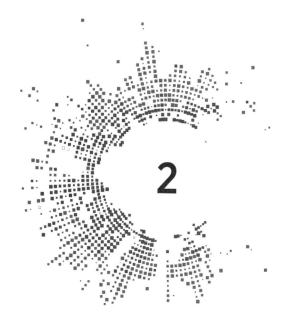

2

Mulligans

What road have you chosen?

The chance to do it over again is called now.
—J. R. Rim

Have you ever had what I would describe as a "do-over" moment? For some of you it may have already happened today. It's the moment when you realize that you should have studied because you're looking at a test and you have *no* idea how to even begin answering the questions. Do-over moments are those times when you just wish you could go back and do something differently.

My friend Walt had one of those moments. Today he is the chief executive officer of Charles Schwab, one of the largest banks and brokerage firms in the world. Founded in 1971, Schwab has over seventeen thousand employees and more than $243 billion in assets. Suffice it to say that Walt has a big job with lots of responsibility, but in college he had a *big* do-over moment.

When Walt was finishing his last quarter of college, one business strategy class required many late nights. The class met two nights a week from 6 to 10 p.m., and throughout those ten weeks he and his classmates often bonded in the halls over snacks as they dreamed of how they would take on the world after graduation. On the day of his final exam Walt and his classmates felt pretty confident that they would ace it after having completed so many business case studies. "We were ready to graduate, thinking we were going to go out and change the world and all be these successful businesspeople," he says. The professor handed each of them a blank white sheet of paper and told the students their final assignment. "I've taught you everything about business strategy as you go into the real business world," he said. "Your final exam is 'What's the name of the lady who cleans this building?'" Walt had no idea. "We had spent four hours a couple of nights each week there for the last ten weeks," he says. "We had taken two or three breaks every evening to get soft drinks or use the restroom, and she had been there every night. I often say to people that I didn't know Dottie's name—her name was Dottie—but I've tried to know every 'Dottie' since."

A popular message suggests, "It's not *what* you know but *who* you know." The idea dates back to a newspaper article in 1914, implying that if you know the right people then things will go better for you, you'll have an advantage, you'll have a better chance at success.

Live*Lasters* know that who you make the time to know is important, but the *who* may not always be so obvious. You might meet them on "the road less traveled."

Without a close second, Robert Frost's poem "The Road Not Taken" is my favorite. Written over one hundred years ago, it has been discussed and debated for years. The metaphor of roads and the choices they represent was not new when Frost put pen to paper, but it's a powerful reminder of the options that face each one of us and the impact of those decisions on our respective lives and those with whom our lives intersect. Read Robert Frost's work again slowly and consider what road you have chosen.

> Two roads diverged in a yellow wood,
> And sorry I could not travel both
> And be one traveler, long I stood
> And looked down one as far as I could
> To where it bent in the undergrowth;
>
> Then took the other, as just as fair,
> And having perhaps the better claim,
> Because it was grassy and wanted wear;
> Though as for that the passing there
> Had worn them really about the same,

And both that morning equally lay
In leaves no step had trodden black.
Oh, I kept the first for another day!
Yet knowing how way leads on to way,
I doubted if I should ever come back.

I shall be telling this with a sigh
Somewhere ages and ages hence:
Two roads diverged in a wood, and I—
I took the one less traveled by,
And that has made all the difference.

Moses understood the importance of the road and reminded all who would hear and read his words of how the road should be used.

Teach them to your children, talking about them when you sit at home and when you walk along the road, when you lie down and when you get up. (Deuteronomy 11:19)

The psalmist offered words of comfort about the road and God's providence in our lives.

God charts the road you take.
(Psalm 1:6 MSG)

King Solomon throws in his wisdom when he warns us about the way we take but then encourages with the words my own mother chose for my life verses:

Trust in the Lord with all your heart and do not lean on your own understanding. In all your ways acknowledge Him, and He will make your paths straight. (Proverbs 3:5–6 NKJV)

We see this picture of a road, a path, a way all through the Old Testament, and then we come to the New Testament, where this powerful picture continues in some even more unique and descriptive ways. Here are but a few examples.

Jesus tells the story of the Good Samaritan. In this story He does something a little unusual in that He talks about a specific place, in this case the road from Jerusalem to Jericho.

It was on this road that a man was attacked, beaten, robbed, and left for dead.

It was on the road to Jericho that Jesus healed a blind beggar who was crying out for mercy.

On the road to Jerusalem, palm branches were waved to honor Jesus.

And Jesus gets personal with words about the importance of roads.

Small is the gate and narrow the road that leads to life,
and only a few find it.
(Matthew 7:14)

I am the Road, also the Truth, also the Life.
No one gets to the Father apart from me.
(John 14:6 MSG)

Jesus makes it clear that we are all on a journey and have two choices. We can take the Jesus Road or we can take the Me Road. One involves sacrifice and surrender. The other invites us to a never-ending pursuit of self. But here's a reminder: whichever road you choose, there will be a host of decisions to make every single day. These decisions are a bit like Robert Frost's two roads diverging in the woods. What will you choose?

On the university campus where I have the privilege of serving, we spend lots of time talking about what it means to live last. Simply described, Live*Last* is a conscious choice to take the road less traveled and act in such a way that it is countercultural. People notice because what you are doing surprises them. We did it one semester when we invited a Domino's Pizza guy to deliver a pizza to chapel. A group of university students pitched in some cash for a guy they had never met and gave him this monstrous $1,200 tip, lots of gift cards, and notes of appreciation. Chad was completely blown away by the generosity. The message that day was one we borrowed from Pastor Andy Stanley:

Do for one *what you wish you could do for* everyone.

Chad was the *one*. He benefitted from a bunch of students who had been encountering pizza delivery guys for years, but that day they took a chance and invested in someone they had never met and might never see again.

In another chapel we gave out a few paper sacks with a random selection of single bills. The challenge was to take the money from the sack, whether it be a one-dollar bill or a one-hundred-dollar bill, and invest in another. The message that day was simply to—

Do what only you can do.

Live*Lasters* understand that as they travel their own unique roads there will be opportunities for service that are special and can be accomplished only if they seize the moment and take a chance. The key is awareness on the road. Who will cross your path today who needs an encouraging word, a smile, or maybe some time?

Jesus had a team who traveled some dusty roads with Him. The Gospel of Mark gives a glimpse of one of those trips:

> *They came to Capernaum. When he was in the house, he asked them, "What were you arguing about on the road?" But they kept quiet because on the way they had argued about who was the greatest. Sitting down, Jesus called the Twelve and said, "Anyone who wants to be first must be the very last, and the servant of all."*
> *(Mark 9:33–35)*

All these years later and some things have not changed one tiny bit. Competition for the top spot on a team, in an office, or in a home is still a temptation. Jesus says the answer is not to argue. In fact, I think He is telling us in a very not-so-subtle way that the way to Live*Last* is to simply—

Do what *no one* else wants to do.

So what is it no one else wants to do?

One thing that no one else seems to want to do is *lose*. We hate to lose, right? Whether it's an argument, a race, a game, or even a parking spot, our competitive juices start flowing and we go all out to win. Though we do not know what Jesus thinks about athletic contests or the challenges of mall parking lots, we can be clear about one thing: He wants us to serve, and most often that means that we may not get the spot closest to the door or the last word in an argument. I'll never forget a lunchtime conversation with a new friend attending a global theology conference in Florida. A mutual friend introduced us and encouraged me to hear this young man's story. It was a fascinating journey from Islam to Christ and it came about as the result of his attending an English-speaking school in Palestine. When I asked him about the reaction of his parents, who are still Muslim, he offered me the counsel he received from his mentor:

Win the relationship, not the argument.

What great advice! What a difference that initiative can make for those who choose a Live*Last* approach on their journey.

Another less-than-popular choice is *sharing*. For most of us it does not come naturally. If you don't believe me, spend some time with two- and three-year-olds. We get older but we still struggle to share. Sharing is what you do on the road less traveled. People notice and they smile.

Something else that no one seems to want to do is *wait*. How about you? I'll be honest with you: I hate waiting! But I remind myself often that Scripture is filled with stories of waiting on God: Noah waiting on rain, Abraham and Sarah waiting on a baby, David anointed as king but then waiting on the perks of the office, even Jesus waiting thirty years before He begins His ministry.

Great things can happen when we wait. Here's something you might try: let someone go in front of you in traffic or in line. You'll be amazed at his or her surprise. Spend some time wondering how you are going to make up the extra three seconds you gave away.

Jesus looked around, and evidently it did not seem that there were lots of people wanting to *serve*. So instead of waiting on others, He got up from the table, girded himself with a towel (the work of a slave in those days), and began washing feet. In those days it was needed, while today, at least in many parts of the world, it is ceremonial. But the message then is as important now. Do what no one else wants to do: serve. Shock your friends, amaze your family, find ways to serve others. Your efforts will be contagious!

One more thing that no one seems to want to do is *forgive*. Exactly what happened when Jesus chose to go to the cross? Talk about doing what no one else wants to do! We are not called to hang on a cross, but we are called to forgive—and the implications are life-changing.

I am reminded of a documentary I saw some years ago on CNN in which reporter Christiane Amanpour interviewed a woman in Rwanda named Iphigenia from the Tutsi tribe. During the Rwandan genocide of 1994 her husband and five children were clubbed and hacked to death by a mob of Hutus, one of whom was one of her neighbors.

The neighbor who had participated in the massacre spent seven years in prison and then went before a tribal court, where he asked for forgiveness from Iphigenia and the whole community. Iphigenia opened her heart and forgave her neighbor. But it did not end there. Iphigenia, a master weaver, also taught her neighbor's wife how to weave baskets. The two became friends and business partners.

On the day that Christiane Amanpour was interviewing her, Iphigenia had invited these same neighbors into her home and was serving them dinner. That's right—she was serving dinner to the man who had killed her husband and children. When asked how she found it in her heart to forgive, Iphigenia said simply, "I am a Christian, and I pray a lot."

Choosing to live last is not easy, but it is possible. Any of us can choose to lose, to share, to wait, to serve, to forgive, but each choice requires us to take the road less travelled.

Questions for Reflection

1. Whom might you seek to win a relationship with instead of an argument?

2. What are you tired of waiting on? Could you make a commitment to wait a little longer?

3. Where might sharing make the biggest difference in the life of another?

Distance

What do you think a Christian looks like?

*Christians—whether as a priest, a nun, a minister, whatever—
have been stereotyped to death. You try to be a model of
kindness and love and forgiveness to those around you,
because you have received kindness and love and forgiveness
from God through Christ. That's what Christianity is.*
—Patricia Heaton

What's your picture of a Christian? If you're honest,
you have an image in your mind. I confess that I
did, though it got interrupted on a flight from Jacksonville to

Charlotte. When I arrived at my window seat near the back of the plane, I found the gentleman on the aisle wearing headphones, appearing to be dancing to the music, with his tray table down even though we were moments away from takeoff. I began thinking that this must be his first time to fly since he seemed not to understand any of the rules or etiquette related to airline travel.

For the previous few days I had spent time at a denominational gathering of ministers, and one of my takeaways was a free book that I planned on reading during the flight. Once the plane had ascended into the sky, I pulled out my theology book and began reading—only to be interrupted by my seatmate, who asked me, "What does sanctification mean to you?" Caught off guard, I asked him to repeat the question, which he was kind enough to do. His question led to a non-stop conversation as we flew to our next stop, where each of us would change planes and continue our trips. My new friend was not only a follower of Jesus but also a professional football player, Rashad Jennings, then a running back with the Jacksonville Jaguars. (He would later play for the New York Giants and still later made an appearance on the television show *Dancing with the Stars*.) Mr. Jennings is a graduate of Liberty University and had a wonderful testimony that he shared with me. Here's the truth:

I misjudged him terribly, because he did not look like a Christian to me.

I've been thinking a lot about what a Christian looks like, or more specifically what a disciple looks like, and I've concluded that it's *not about looks* but rather attitudes and actions. It's about living last.

We don't tend to talk much about disciples, but we do talk about Christians. The New Testament doesn't talk much about *Christians*—only three times is the word used—while the word *disciples* is employed two hundred sixty-nine times. The New Testament is *about* disciples, *for* disciples, and written *by* disciples.

Luke 18 features a parable about two very different but ultimately similar men. It's a parable of contrasts. Jesus liked to show people contrasts: *the first shall be last, when I am weak then I am strong, save your life by losing your life.* We tend to like contrasts because they give us vivid pictures. We like pictures.

The audience for His story that day was a group of people who were confident in their own righteousness and looked down on everyone else. Another way to describe them would be to say, "They were full of themselves." Have you ever known anyone like that? Have *you* ever been like that?

To this audience Jesus told the story of two men who went up to the temple to pray. Both were presumed to be Jewish since Gentiles were not allowed in the temple. But here is where the contrasts began. One was a church-going, tithe-paying, prayer-praying, faithful-fasting, white-hat-wearing individual. The other wore the black hat. He was a traitor, a money-hungry, tax-collecting, slime-in-the-ice-machine kind of individual.

The praying, tithing, fasting, church-going guy *stood up* in the temple and began giving thanks, thanks that he was not like other men—robbers, evildoers, adulterers, or even this tax collector. He was *loud* and he was *proud*.

The other main character in the story hung his head, afraid even to look up to heaven, beating his breast, and prayed, "God, have mercy on me, a sinner."

Perhaps the most interesting thing to me is where this tax collector stood.

> *But the tax collector stood at a distance.*
> *(Luke 18:13)*

Those four words, *stood at a distance,* are only one word in Greek: *makron.* Distance has a way of defining a relationship. We're close to the people we love. All of us have this invisible cone surrounding us that we know as "personal space." When someone violates that personal space, we tend to move away from the person; we're protective of this area. But there are people in your life whom you let violate your personal space. For example, when my daughter was growing up, I ate most of my meals with her in my lap.

Those reading this book who have been around for a while may remember bench seats in a vehicle, and where a young lady chose to sit on a date sent a bit of an unspoken message about what she thought about the gentlemen who was driving.

Close physical proximity is one of the ways we can define a relationship, but it can be deceiving as well. You can sit in a worship service and be miles and miles from God. The truth is that you can sit next to your husband or wife, but because of some issues that are creating tension and conflict, you can be at a distance from your spouse emotionally. The religious man in this story appeared to be closer than the tax collector standing at a distance, but Jesus surprised the audience when He told them that this tax collector was the one who went home justified.

So what's the difference? What's the key to bridging this distance, this gap between you and God and/or between you and someone else?

I think in this parable Jesus gave us one of the most important rules for the race called life. The winning strategy for this life and for all eternity is caring about others. It's letting others go first and not pushing to the front. It's giving without the expectation of getting in return. It's being humble, like Jesus. It's a live-last lifestyle!

Humility opens the door to grace. Now, I'm not sure what picture comes to your mind when you think about humility. I was curious to see what the dictionary offered as a definition. Webster's didn't offer me much insight, defining it as the condition of being humble, or not proud; meekness.

Choosing humility can make all the difference in our relationships with others and with God. At lunch one day a friend gave me a beautiful gold pin with one word on it: *humble*. He told me that I had won this "humble" award. The only problem is that if I ever wear the pin, the award will be taken away from me. I think that's a pretty accurate representation of the challenge of humility.

Some people might think of humility in terms of being quiet or shy or even serving as a doormat. The Bible offers quite a different picture. Jesus teaches us that humility is a pursuit, not a posture.

Again, what is humility? It's that habitual quality whereby we live in the truth of things: the truth that we are creatures and not the Creator; the truth that our life is a composite of good and evil, light and darkness; the truth that in our littleness we have been given extravagant dignity. Humility is saying a radical yes to the human condition.

Humility is not about being in the right place and assuming the right posture. We can fake both of those things. And if you do it long enough I think you can even fool yourself. I believe that's the case with the Pharisee in this parable. He wrongly assumed that his presence in the temple for prayer was what it was all about. He was religious; he thought of himself that way and I'm sure others would have as well.

> *Two men went up to the temple to pray,*
> *one a Pharisee and the other a tax collector.*
> *The Pharisee stood by himself and prayed.*
> *(Luke 18:10–11)*

Before we go any further, I think we need to stop and talk about the difference between humility and self-esteem. Our culture has saturated us with the idea that helping people build greater self-esteem is the most important thing we can do for them. I doubt that's the case. We need to remember that studies show that about eighty percent of the American people believe they are more intelligent, more honest, and more talented than the average person. Now perhaps some of the other twenty percent struggle with low self-esteem, but it's clear that this is not the problem for many folks. Biblical humility is not the same thing as low self-esteem, however. The humblest people I know are people with wonderful self-esteem. Jesus described himself as gentle and humble. Humble people are really those who esteem, or think of, themselves accurately—they just don't think about themselves as often.

A man who I think struggled mightily with humility was Simon Peter. But listen to the words that he would later be inspired to write, words of instruction:

> *All of you, clothe yourselves with humility*
> *toward one another, because, "God opposes the*
> *proud but gives grace to the humble."*
> *(1 Peter 5:5)*

This fifth verse is powerful when you begin to meditate on it. Humility opens the door to grace in relationships with one another and with God. The last portion of the verse was not new from Peter. Solomon wrote those words in Proverbs hundreds of years before. Picture that thought with me for a moment. Do any of you want to sign up to be in opposition to God? Would you like Him in one corner of the boxing ring and you in another? Or do you want His grace poured out in your life?

What's the stumbling block? Solomon gives us the answer and Peter repeats it: *pride.* Pride hinders our relationship with God and I believe also with others. C. S. Lewis put it this way:

> **A proud man is always looking down on**
> **things and people; and, of course,**
> **as long as you are looking down,**
> **you can't see something that is above you.**

Let me ask you a question. Are any of you enjoying absolutely perfect relationships in which there's nothing left to be done?

Could your relationship with God or someone else in your life just continue on without any changes or improvements along the way? I don't think so. I'm also guessing that pride may be the biggest challenge in all of your relationships. It is in mine. *When pride takes over, relationships get stuck.* Communication either escalates or it dissolves. *Humility opens the door to grace, and grace is the bridge that you and I need to make a connection to God and to each another.* Here's another contrast: humility is a lifestyle, not simply lip service.

When asked what were the three most important Christian virtues, one of the early church fathers, Augustine, replied, "Humility, humility, and humility." I think he is still right, but humility is not simply about saying the right words. It splashes over into every aspect of our lives. In a *Peanuts* cartoon Linus tells Charlie Brown, "When I get big, I'm going to be a humble little country doctor. I'll live in the city, and every morning I'll get up, climb into my sports car, and zoom into the country. Then I'll start healing people. I'll heal everyone for miles around. I'll be a world-famous humble little country doctor." Linus sounds too much like many of us. We kind of like the idea of being world famous or at least we want people to know who we are and what we do, but we also want to be considered humble. **I've never met anyone who admitted to wanting to be prideful and arrogant.** I'm convinced that real genuine biblical humility is a magnetic quality. People are drawn to humility. Humility extends the influence of a person. Humble people are like directional signs pointing to God and His grace, but it is an attractive lifestyle, not the words of a sermon. Your favorite people? My guess is that they exhibit great humility.

Remember the contrast between the two prayers in this parable Jesus told. The religious man prayed,

"God, I thank you that I am not like other people—
robbers, evildoers, adulterers—or even like this tax collector.
I fast twice a week and give a tenth of all I get."
(Luke 18:11–12)

Our religious friend was not only a distance from God, but he was also a distance from his Jewish tax-collecting brother. Before you're too hard on him and his prayer, however, stop and do some self-examination. Maybe you haven't stood up in church and prayed something like that, but I'm guessing all of us have had those kinds of thoughts. They come when we start comparing ourselves to other people. The problem is that *other people are not supposed to be our standard of comparison.*

The tax collector in this parable had a little better understanding of the standard. He prayed,

"God, have mercy on me, a sinner."
(Luke 18:13)

I read once of a bicycle race in India in which the object was to go the shortest distance possible within a specified time. At the start of the race everyone queued up at the line. When the gun sounded, all the bicyclists, as best as they could, stayed put. Racers were disqualified if they tipped over or one of their feet touched the ground. And so they would inch forward just enough to keep the bike balanced. When the time was up and another gun sounded, the person who had gone the farthest was the loser and the person closest to the starting line was the winner.

Imagine getting into that race and not understanding how the race works. When the race starts, you pedal as hard and fast as you possibly can. You're out of breath. You're sweating. You're delighted because the other racers are back there at the starting line. You're going to break the record. You think, *This is fantastic. Don't let up. Push harder and faster and longer and stronger.*

At last you hear the gun that ends the race, and you're delighted because you're unquestionably the winner—except that you're unquestionably the loser because you misunderstood how the race is run. Maybe I'm the only one like this, but sometimes I feel as if I'm living in a world where most everyone does not understand how the race is run. They have made up their own rules or have simply adopted a herd mentality and are following the pack. This bicycle race in India seems like a modern-day parable to me where we are competing with each other, trying to push harder and faster, and we've forgotten that the first will be last, the weak will be strong, and those who want to save their lives must lose them.

This parable in Luke is sandwiched in between the story of a persistent widow who kept asking for justice and Jesus is talking about our need to become like children. Both tell me the same thing: God wants us to pull off the masks, to humble ourselves, to be transparent, to quit all the flowery religious talk, and to pray something simple like "Forgive me," "I need help," "Here am I—send me," "Give me strength," or—you fill in the blank.

They don't have to be fancy prayers and they don't have to be lengthy prayers, but they do have to be honest, surrendered prayers.

Let's look at one more contrast. Humility is an assignment, not an alternative for those wanting to live last.

F. B. Meyer said,

> **I used to think that God's gifts were on shelves one above the other and that the taller we grew in Christian character, the easier we could reach them. I now find that God's gifts are on shelves one beneath the other. It is not a question of growing taller but of stooping lower, that we have to go down, always down, to get His best gifts.**

It's interesting to me that when you study Scripture you will discover that humility is not listed as one of the spiritual gifts. In fact, humility is not a fruit of the Spirit. I can't find anywhere in Scripture where we are instructed to pray for humility.

Perhaps what the late Brennan Manning wrote about humility is true:

> **We most often learn humility by being humiliated.**

But listen to what Jesus says about humility:

> *Everyone who exalts himself will be humbled,*
> *and he who humbles himself will be exalted.*
> *(Luke 18:14 ESV)*

If I am reading that correctly, we *choose* humility. It's a conscious decision. In fact, I think it's more than a daily one. I think for some people it has to be almost moment by moment. Some of you might be thinking what I'm thinking—that humility seems to come more easily for some people than for others. And I think you're right. Some personalities, some people as a result of their nature, or maybe their nurture, seem to be more inclined to humility. The reality for most of us is that it's nothing less than a battle—and it's a battle that must be won. Our friend Simon Peter obviously knew that when he wrote,

Humble yourselves, therefore, under God's mighty hand, that he may lift you up in due time. (1 Peter 5:6)

As I pondered this verse, it dawned on me that humility demonstrates a *trust* in God's *timing*. Instead of pushing, shoving, and trying to climb to the top to be first in this race called life, the choice of humility says, "I trust God and His timing." I understand the rules of the race.

I did a life inventory as I thought about this topic, reflecting on some of those moments when I prayed one of those short, transparent, gut-wrenchingly honest prayers like that of the tax collector in this story. I remembered humbling myself by kneeling at an altar in response to a message I heard from a missionary. I trusted Jesus as my Savior for the very first time. My prayer was incredibly uncomplicated: "Lord, save me, please."

Here is what I know about that moment. It was by far the very best decision of my life and I have absolutely no regrets. I also know that I haven't always looked like or been a very good disciple, and though I have preached hundreds of sermons, done the work of a pastor, married, buried, baptized, dedicated, counseled, prayed for and prayed with people, I still remain a work in progress.

Questions for Reflection

1. Who do you know personally who has modeled humility in a winsome and attractive way?

2. What are the ways you demonstrate a discipleship lifestyle for those who are watching you?

3. What is a short prayer you could pray daily to help you live last? Write one.

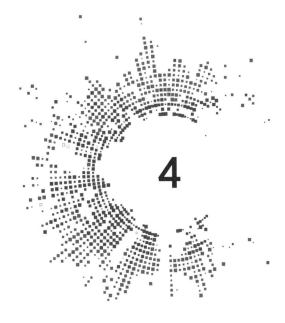

Questions

What's your relationship status?

My great hope is to laugh as much as I cry;
to get my work done and try to love somebody
and have the courage to accept the love in return.
—Maya Angelou

When I was a kid there were no personal computers, no video games, no ear buds, and no cable television—and no, I did not grow up during the Dark Ages. We did spend lots of time outdoors and played games like dodge ball, red rover, and my personal favorite—freeze tag. For those of you not familiar with freeze tag, let me explain. There were boundaries, there were a few rules, and one of the participants was designated as "it." The person who was "it" ran around and used his or her finger like a gun to freeze you. You had to stay in the frozen position until someone who wasn't "it" unfroze you (tagged you so you were free to move again). The other key was knowing where home base was, because there was always a place you could run and be "safe." It was a great game that we played for hours.

I grew older, and in between my freshman and sophomore years of college, when I was 19, I joined the Houston Police Department. I graduated from the police academy and soon found myself patrolling the streets of Houston, playing a more adult form of freeze tag. This time I had a real gun, and the bad guys often didn't know or necessarily obey the rules.

One night early in my career my partner and I were driving down the street, having just made a stop at the donut shop and tanked up with some pastries and coffee, when seemingly out of nowhere a car ran a red light and almost hit our police cruiser. We attempted to stop the car, but the driver decided he wanted to be chased. So off we went at high speeds weaving in and out of traffic, dodging cars both moving and parked. Our suspect turned into an older residential neighborhood with beautiful oak trees in the center esplanade and on either side of the street. It formed a beautiful canopy. We were convinced that he had made a mistake because the street was a dead end. When he got to the end of the street he made a U-turn. We were still in hot pursuit.

As we were approaching the split in the street I noticed from my passenger's side that a garage door was coming up on the far side of the street. Our suspect was headed to the garage where the door was opening. I told my partner what was happening and asked him to stop the car so I could jump out and make it to the garage before it closed. I bailed out and raced for the opening and managed to roll under the door just as it closed. Our suspect thought he had made it home free, not suspecting that I was in the garage with him. I peeked over the trunk of the car and looked through the back window. I could see him looking in the rear-view mirror and laughing. His laughter turned to tears when he stepped out of his car, and I stood up and said, "Freeze!" followed by "You have the right to remain silent . . ."

What he thought was a safe place turned out to be a free trip to jail. Trust me—jail is not a place anyone enjoys spending time in, yet it is a place where the apostle Paul often found himself. He was not familiar with safe places. He was a religious man. In fact, I'm not sure you could have found many who were more religious than Paul. God looked down and decided to humble him in order to use him. A man who was to become the most prolific author of the New Testament was blinded and had to be led into Damascus. It was the beginning of a transformation process that took him from being religious to having a relationship.

I've been religious most of my life. My mother saw to it that we were in church most every time the doors were open. I went to Sunday School and summer camps, sang in the choir, read my Bible, and prayed. Maybe you're in the same category.

The apostle Paul went from being religious to having a relationship and wrote a letter from jail that is generally considered to be his happiest letter. I spent six months in jail once—working, not living there—and I must confess that I never felt like writing anything, but maybe that was because I got to go home every morning when my shift ended.

Here's a verse Paul wrote. I think about it often, and I wonder that if this were true for Paul, how much truer should it be for us?

> I want to know Christ—
> yes, to know the power of his resurrection
> and participation in his sufferings,
> becoming like him in his death.
> (Philippians 3:10)

If anyone should have known Christ, it was Paul, but here at the end of his life he is still expressing the desire of his heart to know Christ better.

There are three questions I believe always get asked in relationships, but seldom are they spoken. These silent questions reflect the deepest longings of the heart. They occupy one's thoughts but are rarely expressed out loud, and they apply to every relationship of life. If you choose to be a Live*Laster*, then your life will be overflowing with relationships. God will send you people to serve, and your service will be a part of the transformation process in their lives. With those relationships will come the following three, often-silent relationship questions:

1. **Can you be trusted?**
2. **Will you love me? (even when I am unlovable, even when I don't love myself?)**
3. **What is the cost?**

Let's tackle these one at a time.

1. Can you be trusted?

I met my wife while I was a detective with the Houston Police Department. I like to tell people that I arrested her and fell in love while I was questioning her about her criminal activity. Some people believe the story until they meet her. The truth is that we worked in the same office, but I had very limited knowledge about her. It stayed that way for a number of months until one night she found out I was in trouble and did me a favor. The very condensed version of the story is that I had a paper due the next day for a college English class I was taking and had procrastinated in finishing the paper—I planned on typing it the night before it was due. (Again, these were in the prehistoric times when we didn't have personal computers). I unexpectedly received an assignment at work that meant I was going to work my normal shift plus all night and part of the next day—and there would be no time to complete my English paper. Carolyn found out about my problem and volunteered to type my paper. What I didn't know then, but has been demonstrated to me many times over, is that Carolyn has a radar for people who are in trouble—and if she can help behind the scenes, then count it done.

In an effort to repay her for her kindness, I offered to take her to dinner the following Saturday evening. The night after our first date she went to church with me where I was serving as a volunteer youth pastor. After church she went with me to a junior high party and we continued to go out every night for, I think, the next eleven nights.

What happened? I wanted to know all about her, and the more I knew the more I wanted to know. I've never asked her, but I guess she felt the same way. And the rest is history. I never asked her if I could trust her and she never asked me, but I promise you that it was a question in our minds. It was not just a question of "Will you be faithful to me?" but much deeper than that: "Can I trust you with my hopes and dreams?"

The apostle Paul had to be asking that question sitting in a house on Straight Street in Damascus as a newly blinded man. I'm guessing he might have been asking it while chained to a Roman soldier as he wrote to the church at Philippi. *God, are You still with me? I've trusted You all this way and I'm not inclined to stop now, but it's only natural to wonder, especially when I'm sitting in jail.*

I found myself asking the *Can I trust You, God?* question as a twelve-year-old boy, when I became the oldest male in my family. Two awful years had seen our family attend the funerals of two grandfathers, both dying premature deaths, one to cancer and the other to a heart attack. We had also lost two uncles, one a young college student on spring break killed by a drunk driver, the other a twenty-nine-year-old Air Force pilot whose plane was lost in the Gulf of Mexico, never to be recovered. The funerals were difficult, but they paled in comparison to the news that my father, a returning Vietnam veteran, had decided to abandon the family—a decision that is still in place even today.

The story is too long to tell completely, but I can say that though those days were the darkest and maybe the most painful of my life, they were a catalyst to move me from just being merely religious to developing a relationship with Christ. I discovered then that I could trust Him. I could trust Him with my pain and even my anger. And over the years I've continued to face times of asking the relationship question: *Can I trust God?* Each time He has proved faithful. I find myself saying, like Paul, "I want to know Christ," even more than I did before.

2. Will you *love* me?

One night my wife and I had a little disagreement and both went to bed mad. I know the Bible says not to let the sun set on your anger, but I did. My wife went to work very early in the morning; in fact, she got up at 4:30 a.m. Whereas I usually get up a little before 6 a.m., she was already off to work. On this particular morning after our disagreement, I got up and started with my morning routine—only I found something unusual everywhere in the house that I went. My wife had evidently cut out little pieces of paper and on each piece of paper was a letter. One of them was taped to the bathroom mirror and another to the refrigerator. One was in my sock drawer and one was taped to the dog food container. There were five letters and an exclamation point. Six pieces of paper in all. When I put them all together I was shocked to discover that they spelled the word *S L I M E!* Now I knew we had had a disagreement, but I didn't think it warranted her calling me SLIME! I left her little message taped to the kitchen counter and headed off to the church that day, doing what any good husband would do: I just ignored her all day. I never called her at work. I just stewed all day long about the fact that my wife thought I was the same thing found in sewers! When I came home that evening Carolyn smiled when she greeted me, which made me even madder. I stewed some more while I changed clothes. When I came back into the kitchen, where she was cooking dinner, she asked me why I had not called her that day. I was all ready with my response: I told her that I didn't think she wanted to talk to SLIME! She very quietly suggested that I take a look at the letters taped to the counter, and when I did I discovered that her message to me was not S L I M E but instead—S M I L E. It even had a little smiley face drawn on the E that I had failed to notice earlier that morning.

I wasn't very loveable then and I'm sure there were some moments before and after when the same could be said, but she meant it when she said those vows: "for better or for worse, for richer or for poorer, in sickness and in health."

You can't predict all the situations you'll need a spouse to love you in and through, but I guarantee that it's a relationship question you'll be asking.

Paul had to have some questions about God's love. What kind of God knocks you down and blinds you? But Paul tells over and over again that his painful encounter with Christ on the Damascus road was a great expression of love. It changed his life forever.

Sometimes we need to be knocked down. When I was in the police academy they talked to us about something called "the John Wayne syndrome." This was an actual psychological term that referred to police officers being convinced that no one could hurt them. The idea is that if you get shot off a horse, you can get right back up and ride again. They warned us that this syndrome showed up in most police officers after they had been out of the police academy about a year. I didn't think it would happen to me, but it did. I look back on that time in my life, and it's painful to remember. But in all my arrogance and status seeking, God continued to love me, as unlovable as I was, and He didn't give up on me because we had a relationship, one He valued much more than I did.

3. What is the cost?

Relationships are expensive, but I don't know anyone who calculates the cost. Can you imagine sitting down with someone you're dating and saying, "I have only thirty-eight dollars to invest in our relationship. I need to know if you're going to fall in love with me before I've spent all the money I've designated." But, of course, it isn't just money. Relationships cost us emotionally and physically.

Our children are both adopted. I had to pay money for them before I ever laid eyes on them. I've spent money on them a lot of days since, but you know what? I love them so much that I never have once stopped to consider what they cost me financially.

There have been moments when I've cried, moments when I've lost sleep, moments when I was so upset with them that I could hardly talk about it. But I knew all that was coming when I decided I wanted to be their father—I wanted that relationship.

In 2 Corinthians 11:23–25 Paul talked about the physical cost of following Christ. He wrote, *I have . . . been in prison more frequently, been flogged more severely, and been exposed to death again and again. Five times I received from the Jews the forty lashes minus one. Three times I was beaten with rods, once I was pelted with stones, three times I was shipwrecked,* and the list goes on. Salvation is free, but it cost Paul something to have a relationship with Christ. But in spite of all that, he stressed, *I want to know Christ.* He spent lots of time in dangerous places but clung to his relationship with Christ.

Do you remember David Bloom? He was a rising star with the NBC television network who went to Iraq to report from the front line during the battle. I knew very little about him other than the times I had seen him on television. You may remember that he died in Iraq. Shortly afterward I was given a copy of an email he had sent from this dangerous place. It was written to his wife, Melanie, a day or so before he died, as he reflected on his life. Listen to his words—because you will hear about the important relationships in his life:

> *Mel,*
> *You can't begin to fathom—cannot begin to even glimpse the enormity of—the **changes** I have been and am continuing to undergo. God takes you*

to the **depths of your being**—*until you are at rock bottom*—*and then, if* **you turn to Him with utter and blind faith and resolve in your heart and mind to walk only with Him and toward Him, He picks you up by your bootstraps and leads you home.** *I hope and pray that all my guys get out of this in one piece. But I tell you, Mel—I am at peace, deeply saddened by the glimpses of death and destruction I have seen but at peace with God and with you. I know only that my whole way of looking at life has* **turned upside down**—*and here I am, supposedly at the peak of professional success—but in the scheme of things it* **matters little** *compared to my relationship with you, the girls, and Jesus. There is something far beyond my level of human understanding or comprehension going on here, some forging of metal through fire. I shifted my book of daily devotions and prayers to the inside of my flak jacket so that it would be close to my heart, protecting me in a way, and foremost in my thoughts.*

When the moment comes when Christine or Nicole or Ava [his young daughters] or you are talking about my last days, I am determined that they will say, "He was devoted to his wife and children and he gave every ounce of his being not for himself but for those he cared about most—God and his family." Save this note. Look at it a month from now, a year from now, ten years from now, twenty years from now. You cannot know now—nor do I—whether you will look *at it with tears, heartbreak, and a sense of anguish and regret over what might have been, or whether you will say—he was and is a **changed man.** God did work a miracle in our lives.*

David Bloom was more than religious—he had discovered a relationship, an intimate relationship. He was living last.

I've discovered in my own life that—

Intimacy is a journey, not a destination.

So, like Paul, I invite you to say out loud to all who will listen, *I want to know Christ—yes, to know the power of his resurrection and participation in his sufferings, becoming like him in his death* (Philippians 3:10).

In the fourteenth chapter of John just prior to the crucifixion, Jesus is having a conversation with His disciples. At one point He says to Philip, "You've been with me all this time and you still don't know Me?"

Could He say to us today, "You've been religious for a long time, attended Bible studies, worshiped in church, even served in leadership positions—but you still don't know Me?"

He trusted us enough to let us choose whether or not we wanted a relationship and, beyond that, how close we wanted the relationship to be. In fact, I would write that you are as close to Christ today as you have chosen to be.

He loves us in our sin, in our unlovable condition.

He paid the price for us.

He's answered the relationship questions.

Questions for Reflection

1. Can He trust you?

2. Do you choose to love Him—even when things aren't going your way?

3. Will you pay the price—whatever that might be?

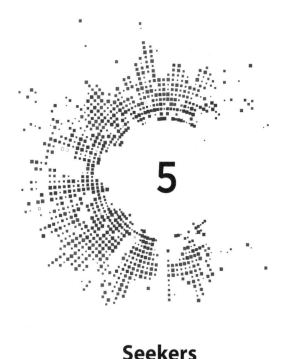

5

Seekers

What's your temperature?

Forgiveness is an act of the will and the will can function regardless of the temperature of the heart.
—Corrie Ten Boom

God's love letter is filled with invitations and one of them is in reference to your spiritual temperature. *Hot* is a pretty descriptive word and one I hear used quite often. Sports commentators describe baseball players who are hitting well as being *hot,* basketball players who are shooting well are described as *hot* too. Businesses advertise *hot* deals. I'm sure there are a thousand other ways the word *hot* is used in which none of them has to do with your actual physical temperature.

A number of years ago I found myself in a spaghetti restaurant on a blind date. Actually it was a double date and I had been set up by mutual friends. While we were waiting for a table, my friend suggested we each put a quarter in a vending machine designed to test one's passion. I had seen how this machine worked and I wasn't very interested in participating. It featured lights and noise and a grip designed to be grasped— and while being gripped it would supposedly test the person's passion. There were lots of options from *red hot lover* to *cold dead fish*, each with corresponding lights and noise that attracted the attention of everyone in the waiting room. Before I could fully decline participation, my buddy had dropped in the required coinage and shoved me in the direction of the machine. The lights blinked, the horns sounded, and my passion had been tested. The results are not important, but let's just say that the machine's verdict was somewhat prophetic about the future of this dating relationship.

Passion is a pretty difficult thing to test. And so is spiritual temperature. The reason? We're so good at faking it. We can fake it in so many ways. People think we have a strong, vibrant relationship with God. We pray before meals, we go to church, we do small-group stuff, but inside we know that our spiritual temperature is a pleasant seventy-two degrees.

You've likely heard the term *assumed room temperature*. For six of my nine years as a police officer I was a homicide detective. I promise you that room temperature is not a good temperature to assume physically. And neither do I think it's a good temperature spiritually.

Jesus had some thoughts about our spiritual temperature.

> *"I know you inside and out, and find little to my liking.*
> *You're not cold, you're not hot—far better to be either*
> *cold or hot! You're stale. You're stagnant.*
> *You make me want to vomit."*
> *(Revelation 3:15–16 MSG)*

Some of the most colorful language in the Bible—the words of Jesus. I read those words and can't help but wonder how many times I've been stale and stagnant and made God want to vomit. Balance those words of Jesus in the New Testament with a wonderful verse of promise from the Old Testament, a verse that has a portion of God's job description in it.

> *For the eyes of the Lord range throughout the*
> *earth to strengthen those whose hearts are*
> *fully committed to him.*
> *(2 Chronicles 16:9)*

God means for us to know something very profound about Him from this verse, and if we understand and embrace the promise of this verse, it can dramatically change our spiritual temperature. If I say to you, "The eyes of the scouts for the Southeastern Conference range throughout the high schools of America seeking to find the best athletes for their schools," you understand that concept because that's what they're employed to do. It's the very nature of a scout to seek and find good athletes and try to recruit them. That's the meaning of a scout.

Verse 9 tells us that it is in the very nature of God to look down from heaven and strengthen those who are fully committed to Him—in other words, people who are spiritually hot. What does it mean to be "fully committed to Him"? How can I keep from being cold or lukewarm?

I looked back at this passage in 2 Chronicles because I was interested in the context of the story. Have you ever noticed how we can pick out verses and memorize them, put them on bumper stickers, inscribe them on stones, but we can't tell what the verses before or after say? Many of us know John 3:16, but we don't know what John 3:15 says. Some of us can quote Jeremiah 29:11–14, but we don't know Jeremiah 29:15.

So I looked at the story that led up to this verse in 2 Chronicles 16:9. What caused the prophet to speak these words?

The message was to the King of Judah, Asa, third king of Judah. He reigned for forty-one years, with thirty-five of those years peaceful. God blessed him, protected him, and prospered him in wonderful ways. In year thirty-six something went wrong and he and his kingdom began a downward slide. He moved from having a heart that was fully committed or hot for God to having a lukewarm and ultimately cold heart.

It reminds me of engravings on two statues that stand outside the National Archives in Washington, D.C.—

What is past is prologue.
Study the past.

King Asa should have studied the past. He didn't and he spent the last six years of his life in misery, spiritually and physically. In year thirty-nine of his reign King Asa was afflicted with a disease in his feet. He went to the local podiatrist but found no help. Ultimately he died, and there's no record in those last six years of his life that he sought any help from God. When I went back and read the account of King Asa I learned some important lessons about spiritual temperature or a heart seeking God.

Great starts don't guarantee great or even good finishes. I did the math and discovered that 88 percent of the time Asa followed God. While 88 percent may be a good grade on a test, God does not define that as a heart fully committed to Him. Asa took over for his dad—that's the way you typically became king—and Scripture says that "Asa did what was good and right in the eyes of the Lord his God." He cleaned up the place, he trusted God, he led his followers to depend on God, he saw God provide for Judah when they went to battle against an Ethiopian army that was twice the size of Judah's. And then Asa decided to take a shortcut. He made a deal with the King of Syria, which was a strategic alliance against Israel.

Have you ever taken a shortcut? I took one in the Rocky Mountains a few years back. I made an ill-advised decision to travel a proposed road in order to save some time and reduce some mileage. I should mention that we were on a family vacation. We were *not* in a hurry. We were not traveling in a four-wheel-drive vehicle, and this was in the days before cell phones. We had a map that I had read—and I promptly ignored it. I should also mention that I ignored my wife's counsel about this shortcut. All in all I was batting .1000!

I should have trusted the map.

Trust your map, this love letter that God has provided. We have an advantage over King Asa: we can read his story and stories like his. We can learn from studying the past.

Another piece of learning from King Asa's story is that God calls us to be transformed. One of our earliest science lessons in school is about metamorphosis. Metamorphosis? I think of the change that takes place when a caterpillar, that bumpy, spiny-looking, worm-like creature encases itself in a chrysalis and is there transformed and comes forth as a butterfly. The difference between those two creatures is about as dramatic as one can imagine, but that is the kind of transformation God has in mind for you if you're going to be a seeker who lives *hot* for Him.

Do you know anyone who is an example for you of what it means to have that elevated spiritual temperature? Living *hot* for God? If you don't, you need to find someone.

Water is transformed at two hundred twelve degrees Fahrenheit. This is the boiling point, at which water begins to change from a liquid to a vapor. Science tells us that. Scripture tells us that we are transformed when we accept God's invitation and allow the Holy Spirit to invade our lives. I don't think King Asa ever really got to the point of transformation. His spiritual temperature would elevate, but it never reached the point of change. He was determined, like a lot of us, to rely on himself and human resources around him.

So how can I be fully committed to God? How can my spiritual temperature be hot?

I read the story of King Asa over and over again, and one thing jumped out at me from God's love letter: God honors and rewards *seekers*!

Such a simple but powerful message! It's a message repeated time and time again in Scripture! Chapters 14–17 in 2 Chronicles reveals the privileges of seeking God and the consequences of failing to seek Him. Jesus comes along in the New Testament and gives us the same message:

Seek first the kingdom of God.
(Matthew 6:33 ESV)

He walked with two disciples on the road to Emmaus, and after spending time with Jesus here is what they asked each other:

"Were not our hearts burning within us
while he talked with us on the road and
opened the Scriptures to us?"
(Luke 24:32)

But you and I are stubborn. We chase all sorts of other things. We are *part-time* seekers. And when we are not seeking, we try to hide. While hide-and-seek was a fun game when we were kids, it doesn't make much sense when we get older. Scripture tells us repeatedly that we can't hide from God and promises us that when you seek Him you will find Him—and your spiritual temperature will be raised. Read this verse again slowly—and then read it again.

For the eyes of the Lord range throughout the earth
to strengthen those whose hearts are fully committed to him.
(2 Chronicles 16:9)

God knows that there are going to be great times in your life and times that really stink, days when you have life by the tail and days when *life* has *you* by the tail. Not every day is going to be the best day of your life, but here's the key: every day can be a day when you are seeking God! You can be seeking Him when you're praying; you can be seeking Him when you're reading His love letter; you can be seeking Him when you come to church— or you can just fake it.

How's your temperature? The regulated body temperature that keeps us healthy is 98.6. It's amazing how God designed our bodies to be regulated there: too hot for too long and we die; too cold for too long and we're dead. But spiritually God designed us to have hearts that are burning for Him. God knows your heart's temperature. He is looking down right now upon you, and His desire is to give you strength if you want it.

When you go to the doctor one of the first things he or she does is take your temperature. It's a part of the doctor's routine in checking your health. I'm convinced that we need a similar routine to check our spiritual health. So set the book down for a moment and take your spiritual temperature. Ask yourself the following questions.

Questions for Reflection

1. Are you cold?

2. Are you lukewarm?

3. Are you seeking these days or doing more wandering?

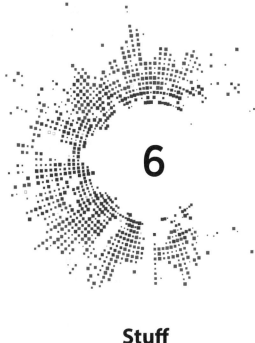

6

Stuff

What is in your inventory?

No one has ever become poor by giving.
—Anne Frank

When I was about thirteen years old I made a trip with my mom, my two brothers, and my sister to our local discount store. It was in the days before Walmart, but it was a Walmart-type store. I was the oldest. My sister was the youngest, three years old at the time. I was way too cool to be hanging out with the family at that point in my life, but my day got worse when my mother decided to buy a plastic swimming pool for my sister. You know the kind I'm talking about—the ones made of indestructible hard plastic, about six feet in diameter, and usually blue. Now the problem from my perspective with this purchase was the fact that we had no way to transport it home. These things are not inflatable or foldable, and I knew it would not fit in our car. At the time we owned a 1964 Volkswagen Bug—there was barely room for *us*! The trunk was in the front of the car so you couldn't put the pool in there and tie it down, because you wouldn't be able to see. I tried to explain this to my mother as we walked through the store, but she just kept saying we would figure something out. I thought she was insane! There was nothing to figure out—it simply could not be done! When we arrived at our car in the parking lot I thought she would finally see how foolish she had been and I with my giant thirteen-year-old brain would be proved correct. But I was wrong—she had a solution. She loaded my brothers and sister in the back seat with the other items we had purchased sitting in their laps, and then she cranked back the sunroof on the VW, put the big blue swimming pool on top of the car, and had me stand in the passenger seat with my head through the sunroof, holding the pool as we drove the five miles home. Keep in mind that this was in the days before seat belt laws—and laws against public humiliation of your teenagers!

Lesson I learned that day: **Make the most of what you've been given!**

My mother taught me that there are two giant questions in life:

1. **Can I trust God?**

2. **Can God trust me?**

As I talk to people about what they've been given, I'm always struck by these same **two things**:

- **What people have been given is not the same.** That may not seem fair, but it's true nonetheless. Look around and you'll see people with great musical ability or the gift of teaching or tremendous athletic prowess or world-class skills in craftsmanship or maybe the knack of making piles of money. Obviously this list could go on and on, but not everybody starts at the same place.

- **People don't necessarily give according to what they have been given.** In fact, it's a fact that sometimes people with the most give the least and those with the least give the most. A case in point is the state of Mississippi, one of the poorer states in the country–but their per-capita giving makes them the most philanthropic state in the United States.

Live*Lasters* are givers who understand the privilege and the joy of sharing, not simply from their overflow but whenever their lives intersect with a need. People study giving patterns, and most of those reveal that we spend much of our life in what could be called the "acquisition" mode and then (and for some people not even then) they move to a "distribution" mode. In other words, they give only when they think they have enough and can spare some of their stuff. The Bible does not teach this model of philanthropy. One of my favorite stories is about one of the youngest Live*Lasters* recorded in Scripture. We don't know his name, but his story is a favorite of preachers and Sunday School teachers. Here is John's version:

> When Jesus looked up and saw a great crowd coming toward him, he said to Philip, "Where shall we buy bread for these people to eat?" He asked this only to test him, for he already had in mind what he was going to do.
>
> Philip answered him, "It would take more than half a year's wages to buy enough bread for each one to have a bite!" Another of his disciples, Andrew, Simon Peter's brother, spoke up, "Here is a boy with five small barley loaves and two small fish, but how far will they go among so many?"
>
> Jesus said, "Have the people sit down." There was plenty of grass in that place, and they sat down (about five thousand men were there). Jesus then took the loaves, gave thanks, and distributed to those who were seated as much as they wanted. He did the same with the fish.
>
> When they had all had enough to eat, he said to his disciples, "Gather the pieces that are left over. Let nothing be wasted." So they gathered them and filled twelve baskets with the pieces of the five barley loaves left over by those who had eaten. (John 6:5–13)

I'm guessing this is not the first time you've read this story. It reads like the tale of a church picnic on steroids except that everyone forgot to bring his or her potluck special. All four gospel writers tell the story: Matthew 14, Mark 6, Luke 9, and John 6. John's version is my favorite because he's the only one who tells us where the lunch came from. Andrew speaks and tells us,

"Here is a boy with five small barley loaves and two small fish."

Notice the facts: five thousand men plus women and children, eight months of wages required to feed this size crowd, and all they have is a boy with a sack lunch—five loaves and two fish. This does not sound like a recipe for success.

Now I don't know about you, but when I read Bible stories I always want to know more than they tell. I want more than just the basic facts. I want some details. For example, the big thing I want to know here is how much more food was in the crowd that day. I'm convinced that there were other people there with food. I can't prove it, but I believe it. I think if I passed offering plates during most worship services, I could come up with more food than they did that day. So here's the Live*Last* question that day and today:

What are you going to do with what you've been given?

They were going to keep it, and that's the answer many people choose to have as they go through life. But there was something different about this boy. For some reason he was willing to give up what he had—all of it. I don't know about you, but I might have been tempted to give them some of it, maybe even half of it, but when it comes to food I'm pretty serious.

One of the first lessons in life we learn is to share. Some embrace sharing better than others. But when we're learning to share, we typically don't have to give up our whole lunch. In fact, it doesn't seem very natural to give away everything.

This boy didn't have much: a sack lunch containing five loaves and two fish. But he did something that day that I believe Live*Lasters* do often. Here's what they do:

- They take an inventory. What do I have? Talent, time, money?

- They consider ownership. Who does it belong to? Is what I have really mine?

- They determine an investment strategy. How can it best be used?

The boy in our story took an inventory and discovered that he had a sack lunch. It wasn't much, but it was something. It was not enough to feed the crowd, not even enough to feed the disciples, but it was what he had. He somehow understood that it really didn't belong to him. Nothing did. When it came to investment, he was willing to take a risk and invest in a possibility. The possibility was that Jesus could do more with the lunch than he could.

So what have you been given? What are you going to do with what you have been given? Where will you invest?

The Bible teaches that God can use *anything* consecrated to Him.

He uses things we waste and things we throw away—crazy things like rocks, water, sticks, mud, spit—and even sack lunches!

The Bible also teaches that God can use *anyone* consecrated to Him.

I don't want to hurt anyone's feelings, but God is not particularly choosy about who He uses. Throughout Scripture we see Him using the old and the young, men and women, Jews and Gentiles, kings and peasants.

As a freshman in college I volunteered for an assignment in my church. A group of boys attended our church from a place called "Boy's Country," but they needed transportation to and from church. Boy's Country was a home for youngsters who, for a wide variety of reasons, could no longer live with their parents. It was located about forty-five minutes from our church. I would drive to church on Sunday morning, pick up the van, drive forty-five minutes to get them and forty-five minutes back. After church I would repeat the process. All of this added up to about three hours of driving every Sunday. One Sunday I went out to get them and found out that they were all gone for the weekend. No one had called to tell me. I drove back to the church and got madder every mile I drove. Freshmen in college value sleep almost as much as anything, and I had given up mine on this particular Sunday for seemingly no reason. When I arrived back at the church, the first person I saw was an eighty-year-old retired preacher. He was my friend, and I started telling him all about it. He listened and then said the strangest thing to me: "Why don't you quit?" I didn't expect him to say that, but it was what I needed to hear.

You see, I thought I was doing the best I could with what I had, but I wasn't doing it for the right reasons. This gift of my time was about me, not about them, and certainly not about God.

Can I remind you that most of what we do in life is *off stage*? Maybe only a few people see it. Maybe no one.

Such was the case in this Live*Last* story about a boy and his lunch. Three of the gospel writers don't even tell us that it was a boy who provided the lunch. John tells us but doesn't give us his name. The boy didn't get famous here on earth, but I think the greatest part of this story is that this little guy got to be a part of a miracle.

Imagine the story he could have told for the rest of his life about the day he donated his lunch.

Throughout history there has always been a two-part process: the *divine initiative* (God's invitation) and then the opportunity for the *human response*. That boy was invited to be a part of a miracle, but he didn't have to. He could have hidden and hoarded his lunch. Either the miracle would not have happened or it would have happened in a different way, but he would have missed the opportunity to be a part.

You don't have to be a Live*Laster*. You don't have to be a part of any miracles. You can hang on to what you have. Keep your talents, your gifts, your resources, your stuff to yourself—or decide that you want to respond to God's invitation and see what He can do with what you have. It doesn't have to be much—five loaves and two fish weren't much—but that little lunch fed more than five thousand people.

What am I going to do with what I've been given?

Here's how I think most people answer the question: "I'm going to wait."

- I'm going to wait until I get more.
- I'm going to wait until it's a better time.
- I'm going to wait until it feels better.

We spend much of our life waiting:

- Waiting to graduate
- Waiting to get married
- Waiting for that first great job
- Waiting to retire

There is nothing wrong with waiting. The Bible seems to put a premium on waiting.

But my challenge to you is simply this: While you're waiting—do everything you can with what you've been given—even if it isn't much! It doesn't have to be much. God plus whatever you have to offer is enough.

Giving almost always involves a risk. We don't know how what we give will be used, and we can't even guarantee that the recipients will be grateful.

What are you going to risk?

Live*Lasters* are risk-takers because they believe that God plus whatever you have to offer is enough.

The story of Don and Joyce still brings a lump to my throat and a smile on my face. Don was a very shy Minnesota farm boy who came to college in 1947. By his own admission he was terribly unprepared to do academic work at the college level. At the end of the first semester the school suggested that he not return, but the story did not end there. Joyce was an excellent student attending the same school, and through what they both would describe as a divine intersection, they found themselves riding a trolley to church in the college town. Joyce took a risk and invited Don to sit next to her on the trolley. When Don was asked not to return for the second semester, he took a risk and got a job as a carpenter in town. Joyce took another risk when Don asked her to marry him. They were united in marriage and then set up housekeeping in a small trailer that Don built. Later, when Joyce graduated from college, they took an even bigger risk by towing the trailer west to southern California where they had been asked to help as volunteer youth workers in planting a new church.

I have a photograph of a world map located in the workshop outside the home that Don and Joyce would eventually move into. I took the photograph of this tattered and faded map with colored pins because of what it *represents*. Pins are scattered across it, each one representing a small school where the Bible is being taught and students are being educated. Most, if not all, of the schools are in out-of-the-way places with limited resources and hungry hearts. In each of these places Don and Joyce had traveled to deliver books that they had purchased or had been donated. Don would build shelving for the books. Joyce would arrange them and catalog them for easy access. This faded and tattered map represented a lifetime of living last.

Some might say that Don and Joyce lived the ultimate love story, and I couldn't disagree, but I might add that I think they demonstrated an exceptional *risk* story and Live*Last* story too!

Remember: you may not get famous on earth for what you do with what you've been given, but eternity can be different if you give what you've been given. The story of Don and Joyce reminds me of the importance of doing what only I can do.

A widely quoted saying states it well:

> *Do all the good you can,*
> *By all the means you can,*
> *In all the ways you can,*
> *In all the places you can,*
> *At all the times you can,*
> *To all the people you can,*
> *As long as you ever can.*

Do that and you will be a Live*Laster*!

Questions for Reflection

1. Where do you find yourself waiting today?

2. If you were going to take a risk, what would it be or where would you take that risk?

3. Make an inventory of all that you have been given and then consecrate it.

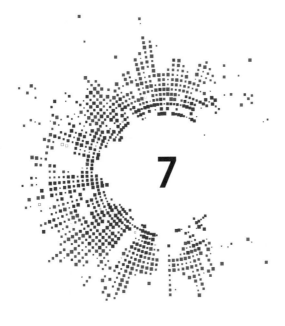

Between

What are you waiting on?

Waiting on God requires the willingness to bear uncertainty,
to carry within oneself the unanswered question, lifting the heart
to God about it whenever it intrudes upon one's thoughts.
—Elizabeth Elliot

Virtually every person I know has spent at least a little time in the drive-through lane at McDonald's. Once I had a very challenging moment there after ordering my large coffee. It was a busy morning, and while waiting I gathered the necessary coins from my right-pants pocket. I needed a dollar from my left-pants pocket, but I had time, so I carefully counted out the coins. All was going well until I dropped a dime, which bounced off of the steering wheel, struck the driver's-side door, and then fell underneath my seat. Since several cars were ahead of me, I thought I had time to retrieve the dime, so I slid my left hand between the door and the seat and felt around until I had secured the dime between my middle finger and ring finger. Carefully I tried to extricate the dime and my hand from under the seat. All was going well until I accidentally struck the power button on the seat with the heel of my hand, lowering the seat on top of my fingers. *Awkward* and *painful* are two words I would use to describe what I was feeling. Things got considerably worse when I realized that I was getting closer to the window where I needed to pay. My left hand was stuck under the seat, I couldn't figure out a way to raise the seat, the driver's-side door could not be opened because my vehicle was up against the wall of the McDonald's, and I couldn't retrieve any cash from my left-pants pocket or my wallet from the pocket of my jacket hanging in the back seat. My mind raced as I tried to consider how I was going to explain to the lady who was holding my coffee and expecting payment.

Have you ever found yourself in a moment when you weren't quite certain what you should do and the clock was ticking? In fact, maybe this moment became extra intense because you were waiting and you didn't know what to do while you were waiting, right?

Jesus had a crew of disciples who were attempting to learn the Live*Last* lifestyle and His time on earth was about to run out with them. He had poured into their lives and was now asking them to get a little uncomfortable as they waited. Though He had told them a number of times that they were waiting on the Holy Spirit, they did not seem to grasp exactly what that meant, how it would happen, or the difference it would make in their lives.

Acts 1 tells the story. Jesus is ascending into heaven, but not without one more set of instructions. He tells them,

> *"Do not leave Jerusalem, but wait for the*
> *gift my Father promised."*
> *(Acts 1:4)*

As I think about that Scripture I wonder if some of the most uncomfortable moments in our lives are those when we're living in the in-between. One event has happened and we're anticipating, maybe dreading, maybe excited about, the next event—but we're "in between."

The word *between* means: **In an intermediate space, position, or time; in the interim**.

Now there's nothing particularly threatening about intermediate space, position, or time, but in my own life I've found those spaces, positions, and times to be uncomfortable. The question to wrestle with is, "How are you going to use this time **in between**?"

If your schedule looks anything like mine, then you have lots of places to be and lots of things to do in this in-between time. And I've discovered that though we complain about our busy schedules, most of us like it that way. In fact, I think society has trained us to be concerned if we don't have something going on all the time.

I have a couple of friends who are living in that time between one job and another. I have several other friends who are living between the doctor's diagnosis and a surgery. And still another friend is between the loss of a friend and the discovery of a new one. One of my best friends is dealing with a prodigal daughter, and he hopes for the moment when she comes to her senses and decides to come home. It's a scary in-between time for him. I'm guessing that some of you can relate to those in-between times.

So what do we do in those in-between moments?

That's a question that people have been asking for years. It's a question that goes unspoken but seems to have been asked frequently in Scripture.

- Noah—One hundred years between the threat of rain and the first drop that fell

- Abraham and Sarah—twenty years between the promise of a baby and the arrival of Isaac

- Joshua and the children of Israel—forty years between Egypt and Canaan

- Joseph—several years in prison waiting for a wrong to be righted

- David—several years hiding in caves between the time he was anointed king and the day he actually wore the crown

- Nehemiah—four months in prayer before he would even dare talk about his burden to rebuild the walls of Jerusalem

- Paul—maybe nine or ten years between his Damascus road experience and his first missionary assignment

- How about Jesus? Thirty years of waiting to begin a three-and-a-half-year ministry

The Bible seems to place a premium on waiting. And I confess that I'm not very good at waiting. Growing up, I was a "package evaluator"—that is, I checked out my Christmas gifts under the tree in an effort to determine what I was getting. My mother got so frustrated with me that one year she marked all four kids' Christmas presents with symbols instead of names. The only problem was that on Christmas morning she had lost her legend, and so we were opening the wrong gifts. My first gift that year was a Barbie doll! I was so confused.

The disciples must have been a bit confused as they stood looking up into the sky. They had been promised a gift and were living in that in-between time. Before we look more closely at Acts 1, I want to take you back to Matthew 28:19.

Jesus says to these same disciples, "Go and make disciples." When someone tells you to go, it's hard to confuse that message, but now Jesus is telling them that before they can go—they need to *stop*.

Have you ever seen anyone try to go and stop at the same time? Years ago I was having my vehicle's oil changed at a business that specializes in this service. A friend owned the business and I was visiting with him as one vehicle was being directed out of the service bay and another one was entering. The entering vehicle's engine began racing, and we could see that there seemed to be a battle going on between the brakes and engine. Something was wrong with the car, or at least the accelerator seemed to be stuck. We watched and wondered what was going to happen. In a fraction of a second the strength of the engine overcame the brakes, and the vehicle struck the exiting vehicle, knocking it out into the street and causing multiple accidents. Thankfully no one was seriously injured, but the picture of the brakes and the accelerator working against each other might give you a good idea of what was going on in the hearts and minds of the one hundred twenty who were living in the in-between. Do we *go* or do we *stay*? I've discovered that many of us are better at going than staying. Waiting simply isn't our style.

Have you ever been chomping at the bit to do something, but it wasn't yet time? When I graduated from the police academy I thought I was ready to go. My fellow cadets and I had been thoroughly trained, but none of it had been the "real thing." We had pretended to make arrests, write tickets, search buildings, and the list goes on. Finally I reported for duty that very first night and while still in the parking lot loading our police cruiser, we received our first call. My partner that night was a twenty-eight-year veteran who had done this many times. I was a rookie who thought he was ready, but as we drove toward that prowler call, I thought I was going to be sick in the front seat. Not a great way to make a first impression! While I thought I was ready to go, I discovered that I was suddenly ready to stay.

The disciples must have thought they were ready to go when Jesus gave them the Great Commission, but then this word from Jesus: *Wait!* The question for the disciples then and disciples now is simply this: Will you trust God's timing in your life?

One of the hardest things for us as humans to do is to wait, since we have such a completely different view of time than God does. Scripture tells us that He looks at days like a thousand years and a thousand years like a day. Paul tells us in Galatians that in the *fullness of time, God sent His Son.* God doesn't wear a watch—it's not that God is not interested in time; it is simply that His view of time is perfect and unhurried, while ours is not. We are people of the clock. Several years ago I had an opportunity to preach the Christmas Eve services in a 22,000-member church in Houston. I was invited back the following summer to preach in their Sunday morning services. I noticed on my return visit that they had installed the largest clock I had ever seen on the back wall of the church in the direct line of sight of the pulpit. I asked if they had done that just for me!

We love timepieces. They're everywhere. My assistant brought me an article once about the message you send to people when you glance at your watch while meeting with them. I think she was trying to send a message to *me.* I confess that I'm not very good at waiting. I'm ready to move on to the next thing. But God says, *Wait—trust My timing in your life.*

The psalmist wrote,

> *I wait for the Lord, my soul waits,*
> *and in his word I hope.*
> *(130:5 ESV)*

Military history records that when the machine gun was invented, there was a big problem. If fired continuously for a period, the barrel would heat up and cause the gun to jam or in some cases explode—not good. In those days there were two simple solutions: you could either change barrels or stop firing for a while.

I think the same can be said about people. Without some periods of rest, refreshment, and renewal, we too can explode. Our souls need to wait and we need to put our hope in His word.

The disciples found themselves waiting for a *gift*. Jesus had spoken about the gift in John 16, but that was several weeks before, and they still thought there was going to be an earthly kingdom. I don't think they understood the possibilities of the gift. I believe Jesus knew that several things would happen as they waited together. Community would be built. Social architecture would be constructed. This group of one hundred twenty would be a core to launch the church. The core of a church gets built only one way—spending time together.

Jesus knew what we know now. It's easier to wait when you're with someone else. If you don't believe me, spend some time in a surgical or intensive care waiting room. People who would never talk to each other out on the street become great friends because of the common bond they share.

For the disciples, the in-between became an opportunity to trust God's timing—just as true now as it was then.

Timing wasn't their only need for trust and it isn't our only challenge either. Jesus wanted them, and He wants us, to trust His plan. Sometimes we're willing to accept the timing but struggle with the plan. Notice the disciples' question and Jesus' response regarding these in-between moments of life.

> *Then they gathered around him and asked him,*
> *"Lord, are you at this time going to restore the kingdom to Israel?"*
> *He said to them, "It is not for you to know the times or dates*
> *the Father has set by his own authority."*
> *(Acts 1:6–7)*

God loves you and has a wonderful plan for your life—and so does everyone else! When I do even a quick review of my life, I can tell you that there have been so many times when God's plan made absolutely no sense to me. I could take you to places where I was more than a little unhappy about His plan, and in my mind there was nothing wonderful about it. But looking back, I can also say that His plan was so much better than mine.

Jesus never told the one hundred twenty exactly how He would accomplish His purpose. He simply told them to stay in Jerusalem. Think about this with me. Jerusalem was not all that exciting a place for them to be. It was the place where Jesus was crucified, and people there were not that fond of the disciples. Verse 12 tells us that they walked down the Mount of Olives— it was on the same road they had taken on Palm Sunday. That was the day they thought they had God's plan figured out. As they walked a little farther on their way back to Jerusalem, they would have passed the Garden of Gethsemane, a place where their idea of God's plan got all confused.

Now they were living in the in-between and were being asked once again to trust God's plan. Maybe you can identify with them. The great news is that God has a plan and when we get off track He is faithful to draw us on a new path back to the highway.

I had an experience once when I was pretty excited about what I thought God's plan was for my life. The day came when I learned that what I had anticipated was not going to happen. When expectations don't match up with reality, disappointment sets in. When disappointment comes, the Bible is a pretty good place to go. On that first day of disappointment I picked up a Bible my mother had left me when she died. She left Bibles for all her children, but I was the oldest, so I received the Bible she had used the longest. Mom was a bit of a pack rat, and her Bible is full of that evidence. One of the things my mother did was choose a life verse for each of her children and grandchildren. Mine was Proverbs 3:5–6: "Trust in the Lord with all thine heart; and lean not unto thine own understanding. In all thy ways acknowledge him, and he shall direct thy paths" (KJV). I read those words on this day of great disappointment, and I confess that I did not feel very directed, just disappointed. Late the following day I checked my email just before trying to get some sleep—disappointment tends to upset sleeping patterns for me. I was surprised to have received an email from someone I don't know well, lived a long way off, and had never sent me an email before. I should also note that though she was about the age my mother would have been, she did not know my mother. In the email this individual acknowledged that she knew I was probably disappointed and offered some encouraging words. She closed her email with the Scripture verses of Proverbs 3:5–6. Coincidence? I don't think so. It was a holy moment in my life. I felt as if God had taken me in His arms and said, *You are My boy! I have a plan for you! It was not what you thought it was going to be, but never fear—I have a plan.*

The timing and plan require trust, but pass that test and you have the privilege of seeing God's power. Jesus gave His disciples a promise for the in-between waiting.

> *"You will receive power when the Holy Spirit comes*
> *on you; and you will be my witnesses in Jerusalem,*
> *and in all Judea and Samaria, and to the ends of the earth."*
> *(Acts 1:8)*

It was the toughest assignment and the most important requirement. It wasn't their timing and it wasn't their plan, and fortunately, it didn't have to be their power. Their responsibility was to wait on the gift, but waiting was not passive—it was active. Remember the prophet Isaiah:

> *They that wait upon the Lord shall renew their strength;*
> *they shall mount up with wings as eagles; they shall run,*
> *and not be weary; and they shall walk, and not faint.*
> *(Isaiah 40:31 KJV)*

Waiting may be the hardest work we do, especially when we're living in the in-between.

The Hebrew word for *wait* always carries with it the idea of waiting with expectation, waiting in hope. The disciples waited and they got power, power for witnessing, power for healing, power for their assignment to *go* and preach the gospel.

I spent some time recently with a chainsaw and for a while it was a chainsaw that wouldn't start. Chainsaws without power are almost worse than useless. It's frustrating to hold a tool in your hands that you know can do the job quickly and efficiently, but with no power it makes you tired just to hold. Finally I got the chainsaw going and made short order of a bunch of fallen limbs in a matter of moments.

The Christian life can be very frustrating when we try to act in our own strength and power. We get tired—tired of waiting, tired of working, and sometimes we get tired and maybe even *sick and tired* of laboring in our own strength and our own power—tired enough that we wait, maybe even in this moment, for God to renew our strength so that we can mount up on wings like eagles.

Some anonymous person wrote this prayer many years ago:

I asked God for strength that I might achieve;

I was made weak that I might learn humbly to obey.

I asked for health that I might do greater things;

I was given infirmity that I might do better things.

I asked for riches that I might be happy;

I was given poverty that I might be wise.

I asked for power that I might have the praise of men;

I was given weakness that I might feel the need of God.

I asked for things that I might enjoy life;

I was given life that I might enjoy all things.

I got nothing I asked for, but everything I hoped for;

In spite of myself, my prayers were answered.

I am among all men most richly blessed.

Can you trust God? This may be life's most important question. I believe you can—His time, His plan, and His power.

Questions for Reflection

1. Who do you know who is living in the in-between and could use someone to sit with him or her for a while?

2. What spiritual discipline might help you while you wait on God?

3. What are some of the lessons you've learned while waiting on God?

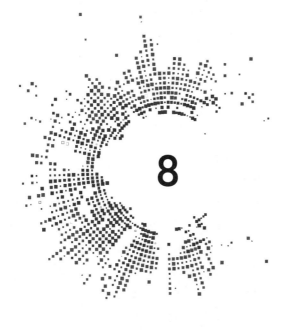

Worms

Who or what is your favorite dynamic duo?

For grace proclaims the awesome truth that all is gift.
All that is good is ours, not by right, but by the sheer
bounty of a gracious God.
—Brennan Manning

For several years the Saturday edition of ABC's *Good Morning, America* program ran a segment where viewers could submit a video clip of their week using only three words. It quickly became a favorite feature of mine. I loved seeing children greeting their military parent with a sign that read, "Welcome Home, Mom" or a cancer patient ringing the bell to a message of "Last Chemo Treatment." Each week I was inspired by the creativity and brevity of celebrating and capturing a person or family's week in three words. It made me think about the challenge of describing a life in a few short words. What would be those words for *your* life?

Maybe a more challenging question is "How would you describe the life of Jesus in only a few words?" Answering that question became important to me when I observed a few years ago that at least a portion of American culture was captivated by the acronym WWJD (What Would Jesus Do?). Bracelets, necklaces, and bumper stickers were only a few of the products asking people to consider what Jesus would do when facing a variety of life's decision-making moments. However, it seemed to me that people needed to know who Jesus was in order to have any kind of clue regarding what He would do.

While reading the Gospel of John one afternoon I gained some insight about Jesus that we need if we're going to choose a LiveLast lifestyle. John tells us this about Jesus:

[He] came from the Father, full of grace and truth. . . . Out of his fullness we have all received grace in place of grace already given. For the law was given through Moses; grace and truth came through Jesus Christ. (John 1:14; 16–17)

Now there are some great dynamic duos in history: Batman and Robin, peanut butter and jelly, Romeo and Juliet, green eggs and ham, and Jonah and the big fish, but I would argue that grace and truth are the greatest dynamic duo ever. When Jesus became flesh and blood and walked the dusty roads of Palestine, people thought they had truth figured out—yet they really had no comprehension of grace. Jesus demonstrated both.

As I look around I'm convinced that our world is desperate for people to be full of both *grace* and *truth*. And I'm convinced that like any great duo, it takes both. One does not work without the other. The challenge is the timing. How many times have you needed grace from someone and he or she gave you truth—or what you desperately needed was truth, but in an attempt to be kind, someone gave you grace?

I met Bill on a golf course playing in a most unusual tournament for charity. The challenge of this particular tournament was the restriction that limited your club selection to one: a five iron. The invitation to play in this expensive fundraiser for a great cause came from another friend, Jim, who asked if I could take the place of his boss, who needed to be out of town on business. On the day of the tournament I arrived at the course only to see that Jim's boss was present after all. A last-minute change of schedule allowed him to participate and forced me into another group with my new friend, Bill. While watching Bill warm up on the driving range I thought this would be a day to remember. Bill was moving lots of earth and his language demonstrated a familiarity with profanity that I had rarely heard, even during my years as a Houston police officer. Jim, by my side for a moment, whispered, "I wish I could be there." My response: "It'll be about the fourth hole." Jim was wanting to be there about the time that Bill inquired about what I did for a living. My experience told me that it would be some time after four or five holes of golf. As we made our way around the golf course, I found myself praying that

Bill would not ask me what I did, because I was confident that when I told him I was a pastor, he would be terribly embarrassed by his language and his behavior. The good news is that Bill appeared to have little interest in me. All the while he told me all about himself. He was an investment banker, quite wealthy with a string of homes scattered in and out of the country. He had married and divorced a number of times with a number of girlfriends in lots of places. As I listened I was reminded of something I had heard before: "The problem with a self-made man is that he worships his creator." Bill gave every appearance of being in love with himself.

After we hit our tee shots on the fourteenth hole, Bill asked the question I had been anticipating. "So Keith, what is it that you do when you aren't playing in charity golf tournaments?" After thinking about it for these past few hours, I thought I had the appropriate response: "I'm in the investment business." "Really?" Bill responded. "What kind of investments? Real estate, stocks, bonds, commodities?" "No, none of those, Bill. I'm involved in eternal investments." Bill gave me the strangest look and said, "I've never heard of those!" For the next few minutes I talked to Bill about Jesus and the joy and freedom of a personal relationship with the one who knows us best and loves us most. While I would love to tell you that Bill was interested and full of questions, the conversation ceased in our golf cart and we played the last few holes in silence. As we shook hands at the conclusion of our round and went our separate ways, I was reminded of how many people there are in our world just like

Bill. They will need someone to extend lots of grace to them, and we need to be fully prepared to talk to them about the way, the truth, and the life, Jesus.

Grace was and is God giving himself to us in Jesus.

> *The Word became flesh and made his*
> *dwelling among us.*
> *(John 1:14)*

Giving us Jesus was not God's first act of grace. Creation, relationships, freedom of choice, manna and quail—the list of grace-giving acts goes on and on. The greatest gift of grace is salvation, and it is a gift available to each of us.

> *It is by grace you have been saved through faith—*
> *and this is not from yourselves, it is the gift of God.*
> *(Ephesians 2:8)*

But salvation is not the only grace we have received, are receiving, or will receive. I love this quote from Jerry Bridges:

> **Your worst days are never so bad that you are**
> **beyond the REACH of His grace. Your best days are**
> **never so good that you are beyond the NEED of God's**
> **grace. Every day should be a day of relating to**
> **God on the basis of His grace alone.**

Grace is only half of the dynamic duo, but it's the one that often seems the easiest to embrace. Yet truth is necessary for us to truly understand, accept, and celebrate the grace God gives so freely to us. Truth is God revealing himself to us in His Son, Jesus Christ. Again, the Gospel of John gives us the story.

> *We have seen his glory, the glory of the one*
> *and only Son, who came from the Father.*
> *(John 1:14)*

Our world wants to tell you that there is no real truth, that you just make it up as you go, and that all roads lead to heaven, but that's not what the Bible teaches. Twenty-eight times the Gospel of John records Jesus as saying, *I tell you the truth*. Jesus came not only to tell the truth but also to *be* the truth. Truth becomes the measure against which all human behavior must be judged. The challenge is what we do with the truth. Truth can be believed or denied, accepted or distorted, obeyed or rejected, celebrated or hated. The interesting thing about it is this: no matter what you feel about the truth, it does not change the truth.

As a former police officer, I like to use the illustration of the automobile. While it may be able to travel in excess of one hundred miles per hour (something I do not advise), the truth is that practice will find you exceeding the speed limit. If you find yourself trying to answer the question "Why were you speeding?" you know that various responses like "I didn't know the speed limit," "My passengers encouraged me to drive this fast," "It's the manufacturer's fault for allowing the car to travel at this speed," "I felt like it," or "I don't agree with the speed limit" will not be adequate. In those moments you'll need a law enforcement officer who's willing to extend grace to you.

Truth is timeless and is to be taught. Harvard University began as a school to prepare ministers. In those early days the university seal contained the motto in Latin: *Veritas Christo et Ecclesiae,"* which means "Truth for Christ and the Church." When I read this motto, the Scripture quotation from John 8:31–32 comes to mind, the words of Jesus:

> *If you hold to my teaching, you are really*
> *my disciples. Then you will know the truth,*
> *and the truth will set you free.*

When I think about the best teachers, the best professors I've ever had the privilege of learning from, I realize that they were women and men of truth and grace. Grace is God giving himself to us. Truth is God revealing himself to us. Jesus came from the Father full of grace and truth, and if a Live*Last* life is a person's choice, then grace and truth must be his or her commitment.

I'm convinced that grace and truth go hand in hand— they're the ultimate dynamic duo. One does not work without the other. In fact, without truth I can argue that no one needs any grace, because then everything is acceptable. But with truth, grace becomes indispensable since we all fall short. Here is the problem: Sometimes we need grace and what we get is truth, and there are times when we need truth and what we get is grace. If we can understand the way grace and truth are to be lived out, I think it will dramatically change the way we deal with our children, our spouses, our friends, those people we work for and work with.

When I study the life of Jesus I find that He provided a very simple model: Grace always precedes truth, but truth is never left out of the equation. Do you remember His encounter with the Samaritan woman at the well in John 4? His very presence and conversation with her demonstrated multiple acts of grace. In that culture and at that time Jews and Samaritans did not associate with each other and most certainly would not have been engaged in a conversation—and yet there Jesus was, by choice, talking to her about her life. The moment of truth came when He asked about her husband. Consider what the story might have been like had He led with the question "Where is your husband?" One chapter later in John's gospel Jesus encountered a man who had been an invalid for thirty-eight years. The grace moment was when Jesus asked him if he wanted to get well, but read on in the story and you see a truth moment when Jesus confronted him with the words "Stop sinning or something worse may happen to you" (John 5:14). These are but two examples of the consistent message of Jesus to lead with grace and confront with truth—a powerful practice of Live*Lasters*.

May we understand that timing is critical as we attempt to navigate the complexities of relationships and the dynamics of personalities. There is a time for truth and a time for grace, and that timing is not interchangeable.

For some of us, because of our personalities or the environment we grew up in, grace comes much more easily than truth. For others it is just the opposite in that we are much more comfortable with truth than grace. It's critical to understand that we need both to be operating in balance in our lives if we are going to fulfill our call to imitate Christ and influence others.

The Old Testament story of Jonah, a favorite for many, offers another portrait of this dynamic duo of grace and truth. Ask someone to complete this duo: Jonah and the _____ and I can almost guarantee he or she will fill in the blank with the word *whale*. After all, that's the way we heard it in Sunday School. Yet there was another character in that story that deserves some attention. The whale—or leviathan or great fish—rescued Jonah when he was drowning, an act of grace, wouldn't you say? Read a little further in the story and you will discover another character that becomes instrumental in Jonah's life. While the whale represents grace given to Jonah in a moment of extreme need, the tiny worm of Jonah chapter four provides a truthful correction that was every bit as significant. Grace and truth come in different shapes and sizes designed specifically for our needs, but never forget that we need both and are called to extend grace and stand for truth.

Questions for Reflection

1. Is there someone who really needs grace from you— but what you're giving him or her is truth?

2. Is there someone who really needs truth from you— but what you're giving him or her is grace?

3. Is there some grace or truth you need to give yourself?

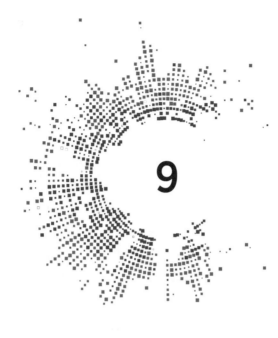

Decisions

What are you hungering and thirsting for?

The hunger for love is much more difficult to remove than the hunger for bread.
—Mother Teresa

For a number of years I was privileged to work in a building that featured a bookstore, coffee shop, post office, health center, hair salon, cafeteria, and a Chick-fil-a! Sounds like a dream, doesn't it? One day I walked past the Chick-fil-a and saw a sign advertising their milkshakes. I've never had one of their milkshakes, but there was something so tempting about that idea that I had to force myself to continue on upstairs to my office without stopping. For some reason I had a hunger and a thirst for a milkshake and I wanted to be filled. I confess that I've not always been so disciplined.

Full stomachs have a way of making most of us happy, happy, happy! Did you know that experts tell us that when a baby is born, he or she has one impulse, one drive, one instinct: to nurse? Before the newborn is cleaned, wrapped, or cradled, his or her mouth begins to root for that which will bring contentment. Brand-new babies find rest and contentment when they find the nourishment they need for life. And if you've spent any time around babies, you know they'll let you know when it's time for their bellies to be filled!

Jesus speaks about a different kind of hunger and thirst.

> *"Blessed are those who hunger*
> *and thirst for righteousness,*
> *for they will be filled."*
> *(Matthew 5:6)*

How does this verse make you feel?

Think about it for a moment with me. Soak it in. Meditate on it. Everybody I know is hungering and thirsting for something. Take out the words *righteousness* and *filled* and leave them blank for a minute. Whatever you put there determines the end result.

Imagine this:

- Blessed are those who hunger and thirst for *Big Macs*, for they shall be *large*.

- Blessed are those who hunger and thirst for *entertainment,* for they shall be *bored.*

- Blessed are those who hunger and thirst for *acceptance,* for they shall be *needy.*

So here is my question for you: What are you hungry and thirsty for? How is that working out for you?

Isaiah offers a poetic commentary on this beatitude when he asks,

Why spend money on what is not bread,
and your labor on what does not satisfy?
(Isaiah 55:2)

The entire book of Ecclesiastes is Solomon's search to determine what is most important in life, what brings meaning. Jesus answers it for us here in Matthew, but it's not an easy answer. He says, pursue *right-ness,* or *righteousness,* or *holiness.*

If we choose a Live*Last* lifestyle, then we must hunger and thirst for righteousness. Why? Well, I've determined that our desire influences our decisions. Makes sense, right? If my desire for food is greater than my desire for health, then I'll spend more time in restaurants than on a treadmill or a bicycle! If my desire for education is greater than my desire for inspiration, then I'll spend more time in a classroom or library than on the side of a mountain or in a park. Desire is powerful, and I remind you that it is God-given, which makes it a gift. So the problem is not desire.

Remember the words of James:

God cannot be tempted by evil, nor does he
tempt anyone; but each person is tempted when they are
dragged away by their own evil desire and enticed. Then,
after desire has conceived, it gives birth to sin; and sin,
when it is full-grown, gives birth to death.
(James 1:13–15)

So the problem is not desire—it's the decisions we make based on desires. My friend Ron Blue has a line I love and use often:

The longer the perspective, the better the decision.

Think about that. If you decide in the spur of a moment (and many people do), there's a good chance it may not be the best decision. I have some friends who made a quick decision about the purchase of a new car. When they got home and started thinking about what they had done, they had buyer's remorse. The next day they took the car back and tried to retrieve their old car, but it was too late—their old car was gone. They ended up turning the new car in and purchasing another one, but it cost them extra. Now, what happened to them has probably happened to all of us. Anyone make a decision that you regret? I have a list!

What if you made all your decisions based on an eternal perspective? Here's what I think would happen:

- It could radically alter some of the biggest decisions you make in life.

- It could give you a peace that allows you to rest in His peace instead of worrying.

- It would make you a person whom other people would seek out to find wisdom.

- It would make you different than most of the people in this world.

I love this verse:

> *Delight yourself in the Lord, and*
> *he will give you the desires of your heart.*
> *(Psalm 37:4 ESV)*

How do we delight ourselves in the Lord? We spend time in His Word—talk about an alteration of your perspective. We seek ways to serve His people—this can't help but change you. We resign as ruler—it's not about my way; it's about *His* way.

Joshua reached a moment when he called out the children of Israel and told them to examine their desires and make a decision.

> *"Choose for yourselves this*
> *day whom you will serve."*
> *(Joshua 24:15)*

What happens next? The progression is a logical one. Our decision impacts our direction. So you decide, and that charts your direction. While there are always risks involved since no one has the ability to see the future, the ability to decide is a gift. Even the emperor Napoleon understood the challenge and privilege of making decisions. He said,

Nothing is more difficult, and therefore more precious,
than to be able to decide.

We face at least three different kinds of decisions.

1. Rational/Analytical—these are the decisions that are hopefully thought through, researched, discussed, contemplated, and prayed over. Some examples might include the choice of a university, the choice of a spouse, the choice of a career

2. Intuition/Gut—all sorts of options here, but some examples would be about which restaurant to visit, what movie to go see, where to go for vacation

3. Random—even more options in this category, but some examples might be what you order in a restaurant, the television show you choose to watch, or which line to stand in at the grocery store

Researchers suggest that we make up to thirty-eight thousand decisions every day, but what might happen if we make random decisions about things that should be analyzed or if we spend tons of time studying what should be a random decision?

What about your decision to trust Christ as your Savior? Rational/Analytical? Intuition/Gut? Random? It could be any of the three or a combination of the three, but once you decide, then the direction of your life changes. No one likes to talk about hell much anymore, but the Bible teaches it so I believe it's okay to speak and write about it. When you make a decision to trust Christ, your direction is not hell but heaven. However, the decision should not be just about eternal life but this life here as well.

My wife, Carolyn, and I were both homicide detectives with the Houston Police Department when we met. Though we had worked in the same building for several years, we had been assigned to different divisions and worked different shifts, so we were completely unaware of each other. But then at 61 Riesner, on the third floor, working the evening shift in the Homicide Division, we became acquainted. Meeting her ultimately changed the direction of my life—for the better, I might add.

Now being a homicide detective is a really weird job in that your clients are typically dead the first time you meet them, but then your job is to learn all you can about them. So how do you get to know a dead person? You look at his or her desires and direction! Quite often you learn about that by looking at the person's calendar, checkbook, credit card statements, and cell phone records. True for the dead person, true for you and me too! How much time did you spend in God's Word this past week? How often did you call home and talk to the Father in prayer? Are you generous with God and others, or are you hoarding money for yourself?

Show me how you spend your money and your time, and I'll show you your desire and decisions, and I can chart your direction.

Jesus had another statement in the Sermon on the Mount that I think often relates to His subject. He said,

"Where your treasure is,
there your heart will be also."
(Matthew 6:21)

Note: He did *not* say, "Where your heart is, there your treasure will be." Go on a treasure hunt—find your heart.

Here's another thought about decisions.

"No decision" is itself a decision.

For those who say, "I'm not sure about this whole Jesus thing—I'm just going to wait and see how it all works out"—I want to remind them that *no* decision is a decision itself.

A number of years ago I was flying from Houston to Dallas, then on to Wichita Falls, Texas. I was seated by the window and the gentleman next to me on the aisle was extremely nervous, so nervous in fact that he began to make *me* nervous. He just couldn't seem to sit still, and as he continued looking out the window (invading my personal space), I began to get irritated with him and imagined all kinds of scenarios. I wondered if he was a hijacker or if he knew something about the plane that I didn't know. Finally he began talking to me and apologized for his behavior. He told me that he hated to fly. I asked him how often he flew, and he responded, "Every single week!" He was a salesman and his job required him to fly often. As we talked about flying he made a statement that I've never been able to shake. He said, "If I could just know the pilot, I think I would be all right." I understood what he was saying, because I believe that if you can just meet Jesus, then you'll begin to hunger and thirst for righteousness—and the promise is that you'll be filled!

One more thought about this decision-making process.

Direction determines destiny.

Nothing new here—show me your direction and I'll show you your destiny.

Jesus has great advice for us:

> "Seek first his kingdom and his righteousness,
> and all these things will be given to you as well."
> (Matthew 6:33)

How is your hunger and thirst for His kingdom and His righteousness? It's a question of priorities. Get the priorities right and you get everything else right too!

The author of Hebrews was writing to a group of Jewish Christians who were considering changing their direction. They were wanting to give up and go back to looking for another Messiah, because times were hard and Christians were being persecuted. The author recounts the stories of faith in chapter 11 and then challenges them in chapter 12:

> Therefore, since we are surrounded by such
> a great cloud of witnesses, let us throw off everything
> that hinders and the sin that so easily entangles. And let
> us run with perseverance the race marked out for us.
> Let us **fix our eyes on Jesus**, the pioneer and perfecter of faith.
> (Hebrews 12:1–2)

When I get in trouble with my desires, my decisions, my direction—it's because I've taken my eyes off of Jesus. **I've**

quit hungering and thirsting for right-ness. Jesus gives us perhaps my favorite story in the New Testament, found in Luke 15:11–31. We know it as the story of the prodigal son. There are several characters in this chapter, but the focus is on a son who was hungry and thirsty for all the world had to offer. Ultimately he made a demand and later rehearsed a request.

His demand was for "his money." Do you remember how that worked out for him? Not too well, as he ended up so desperate for food that he wanted to eat what the pigs were eating. I think he was also hungry for family, so he decided to make his way home in hopes of at least finding a place where his stomach could be filled. Along the way (returning from a path that he had chosen for himself but was never the desire of his father), he rehearsed a speech. He was going to ask his dad to make him a servant. Read the story again, and you'll see that he never got a chance to ask to be made a servant. His father made a decision and called for a celebration. The destiny of his lost son had changed! It's a story of grace—which is the ultimate message of Jesus.

I love these words from Max Lucado: "*Grace* is God as heart surgeon! Grace is God cracking open your chest, removing your heart, poisoned as it is with pride and pain, and replacing it with his own."

When we choose to live last, we choose to serve, we choose to hunger and thirst after righteousness, we choose to follow the path God has prepared for us.

Questions for Reflection

1. Spend some time with your checkbook, your calendar, and your cell phone. What message would these records send about your life?

2. Who do you know who models hungering and thirsting after righteousness best? Make an appointment to spend some time with this person and learn all you can.

3. Read Luke 15:11–31 every day for a week. Henri Nouwen says that at some point in life we will be every character in this story. Which character does your life most represent right now?

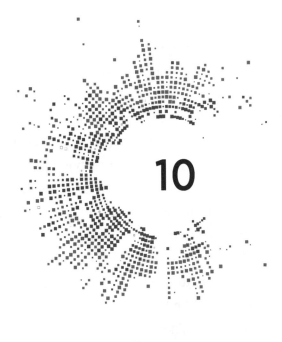

Teams

Who steals your sleep?

*The purpose of human life is to serve and to show
compassion and the will to help others.*
—Albert Schweitzer

Fishing brings me great joy—and I don't do it nearly enough. I saw a T-shirt on a man recently that said simply, *I Fish, Therefore I Lie,* which reminded me of this prayer: *Oh, give me grace to catch a fish / So big that even I / When talking of it afterwards / Have no need to lie.* With that in mind the story I am about to tell you is true, and I have a witness—but keep in mind that he too is a fisherman and a pastor.

My pastor friend was even more passionate about fishing than I am. We had been living in the same city for only a short time when we discovered our mutual affection for the pursuit of these scaly and smelly creations of God. He came up with a plan to take a trip to a lake a couple of hours away. It was at a time in my life where I was really swamped and was not sure I could even afford a night and a day away to fish, but my friend was insistent and persuasive. He went to great lengths to borrow a boat, find a place to stay, and make all the other arrangements. I was convinced that he had done all he could to insure a great time of fishing, right down to having a special time of prayer the night before we were to hit the lake. All the plans seemed wasted when he backed the boat down into the water and I attempted to start the engine. Our borrowed boat had been sitting for a number of months, maybe years, and when I stood up in the boat to check the engine, the steering wheel snapped off in my hands. I quickly tried to stick it back on, not wanting to disappoint my friend, but it was simply symptomatic of other problems the boat had. It seemed our fishing trip was doomed to be a failure. By the time we got the boat put away, the sun was high in the sky, and we stopped by the marina to try getting a little local knowledge of where we might fish off of the bank and have some success. We were directed to a spillway, an overflow of the lake, and upon our arrival we saw that there were more people there than there were out on this large lake. Finding our spot, we began fishing—and over the course of the next seven or eight hours, we caught fish on virtually every cast and sometimes two fish at one time.

I learned lots of lessons on that trip, but probably the biggest was the importance of going where the fish are biting. It's so much easier and so much more fun.

Jesus said to the first disciples He called, "Come, follow me, and I will make you fishers of men" (Mark 1:17, author's paraphrase), and later just before He left them to return to heaven He said, "Go and make disciples of all nations, baptizing them in the name of the Father and of the Son and of the Holy Spirit, and teaching them to obey everything I have commanded you. And surely I am with you always, to the very end of the age" (Matthew 28:19–20).

In short, I think you could say Jesus gave us instructions something like this: *Go fish!*

How do we do that, especially in a society where it seems as if the fish are not biting very well? Do we give up on the United States and simply determine that we are living in a post-Christian, immoral society that is destined to continue deteriorating? Or is the Great Commission still *our* commission? Do we see it as a *burden,* something we have to do, or a *blessing,* an assignment we are empowered to fulfill?

Years ago I was given a book written by Ken Blanchard and Don Shula. The authors begin by stating that if organizations want to be successful or, in my paraphrase, would want to fulfill a commission, they need to be conviction-driven. In other words, what do we stand for?

I think that's how we fish, and I'm convinced it works regardless of the society or culture we live in.

Mark 2 begins with the story of four Live*Lasters* who go the extra mile and the decision had a dramatic impact on the life of a friend. We are given few details, but we learn in this story that to be a Live*Laster* you have to move beyond feeling and beyond talking about your feelings. Live*Lasters* seize the moment, make the most of every opportunity, and refuse to settle for the status quo.

Two words define what these four Live*Lasters* did. The first definition is—

**COMPASSION—*sympathy for the suffering of others,
often including a desire to help***

Without question Live*Lasters* are compassionate people; they have sympathy for the suffering of others, and often that includes a desire to help. You see that in these four men, but there's a second definition that's important as well—

**ACTION—*the process of doing something in
order to achieve a purpose***

Put the two words together and you get the word *compaction*, but not the geological definition. Compaction is doing more than feeling sorry for a person, going beyond expressing your sorrow to him or her—it is reaching out with the purpose of making things better. Scripture does not give us the names of the four Live*Lasters* in Mark 2, but I believe they were men of compaction, and as we look at their story I think we can learn more about what it means to be a Live*Laster*.

Live*Lasters* take an inventory to determine what they have been given. I've never worked anywhere that required you to take an inventory, but I've known people who had that assignment as a regular part of their monthly routine. Each month they generally had to stay late and take stock of all their company had. Reports were generated; sales and surplus needed to balance. Taking inventory is time consuming but an important time for many businesses. When I read this story, I'm convinced that these four guys did a similar thing—they took inventory. Perhaps they considered how blessed they were and were reminded of the need of their friend. Scripture tells us—

Some men came, bringing to him a paralyzed man.
(Mark 2:3)

This is one of those stories that I would love to know more about. Had one of them met Jesus? Had all of them heard about Jesus? Was the idea of picking up their paralytic friend and carrying him to Jesus the idea of one of them, or did something happen that led all of them to compaction?

One of the things I love about this story is that these guys were blooming where God had planted them. They took an inventory and discovered that they had a friend with a physical need—and they practiced an early form of networking. They had an idea that if they could connect the need with the right resource, something amazing could happen.

When was the last time you took an inventory in your own life? Think about where God has planted you. Who are the people in your life and what are their needs? Where are the resources that might meet their needs? How could you connect the resource with the need?

Paralysis is the obvious need in this story in Mark 2, but Jesus saw a deeper need. In fact, He healed the spiritual need before He dealt with the physical need, but it didn't have to be that way. Sometimes we meet physical needs or financial needs in an effort to establish a relationship and build a bridge so that we'll have the opportunity to see a spiritual need met.

God created us to be in relationship with other people, and He knew that we could use the influence of those relationships to see the kingdom multiply. We are the only plan. God has always used people to reach people, and in doing so the kingdom is multiplied. It can start by taking inventory of the people in your life.

The LiveLasters in this story decided to do a really healthy thing—they teamed up! Our four friends in this story teach me that it is not necessary to have the gift of evangelism in order to be a LiveLaster. All you need is some time, a few muscles, a mat, a little faith, and a lot of love. Mark tells us that the paralytic was—

carried by four of them.
(Mark 2:3)

What if one of them had been busy that day or thought it was a bad idea or didn't agree with the plan? Here's my favorite definition of a team:

A group of interdependent people committed
to a common purpose who choose to cooperate in
order to achieve exceptional results.

I would say these four life-givers qualifed as a team.

Isn't it true that we can do so much more when we team up? Whether with a few friends, a small group, or even as a whole church, exceptional results are the possibility when we work together.

I love the story of Herman Ostry's barn. It seems his barn floor was under twenty-nine inches of water because of a rising creek. The Bruno, Nebraska, farmer invited a few friends to a barn raising. He needed to move his entire seventeen-thousand-pound barn to a new foundation more than one hundred forty-three feet away. His son Mike devised a lattice work of steel tubing and nailed, bolted, and welded it on the inside and the outside of the barn. Hundreds of handles were attached. After one practice lift, three hundred forty-four volunteers slowly walked the barn up a slight incline, each supporting less than fifty pounds. In just three minutes the barn was on its new foundation.

There's something quite rewarding and energizing about accomplishing something as a team. I don't think it was an accident that Jesus chose disciples. They were diverse, at times difficult—but I believe He knew that when He returned to heaven, they needed to understand the importance of what could be accomplished when a group works together.

Our LiveLasters in this story took a risk. I think this paralytic was blessed to have the kind of friends he had. They were willing to take a big risk, a huge risk. Risk makes us vulnerable and risk has the possibility of rejection. And the truth is that taking big risks requires courage because there's the potential for failure. Someone has said that courage in people is like a tea bag. You never know their strength until they're in hot water. Look at what happens in this story:

> *Since they could not get him to Jesus because*
> *of the crowd, they made an opening in the roof*
> *above Jesus by digging through it and then lowered the*
> *mat the paralyzed man was lying on.*
> *(Mark 2:4)*

A typical Palestinian roof was flat; in fact it was often used for sleeping. It was reached by an outside stairway or ladder. Roofs were made of earth and brushwood that were packed between wooden beams set about three feet apart. It would have been pretty bold and brazen to climb up on a roof and then begin tearing a hole in it.

In our litigious society can you imagine the lawsuits and the OSHA investigation that would have taken place because of what these guys did?

I like this part of the story because these guys were innovative. No one had ever done it that way before! And I can envision the possibilities of an argument that could have developed right there because they had never done it that way before. I think it would have been easy to have said, "We tried, but it's just too crowded in there. Maybe we can catch Jesus on a day when He's not quite so popular." But they didn't let the obstacles deter them.

Steve Sjogren started a church in Cincinnati with five people. He became a Christian in southern California during the Jesus Movement. About his salvation experience he writes, "Evangelism in those days was like fishing during a salmon run

. . . about anyone with minimal availability could catch fish." But he continues, "Today we are no longer fishing in a salmon run." During the first thirteen months in Cincinnati he shared his vision for planting a church with a thousand people, but on his first Sunday only thirty-seven people showed up, many of them from out of town who came to wish him well. He joked, "That's enough rejection to give Norman Vincent Peale a challenge." In those early days of discouragement he felt God speaking to him about taking a risk and trying to reach people a different way. They started doing some strange things, like—

- Mowing people's grass (with their permission, of course)

- Wrapping gifts during the Christmas season at a local shopping mall for free

- Giving out cold drinks to people stuck in traffic trying to get into a Reds baseball game

- Washing cars for free, refusing to accept even donations.

Some of the things they have done are even stranger, but each of these has been done with the attitude and the message: *Jesus loves you.* They were not trying to stick religion down anyone's throat—just wanting people to know some people out there had taken inventory of their community, teamed up, and were willing to take a risk because the possibility of their salvation made it worthwhile. Sjogren's church grew to thousands of people, many of them who first became acquainted with the church because someone offered them an unexpected gift with no strings attached.

The Live*Lasters* in this story trusted God in a very big way. It sounds obvious, but I'm not sure it is. The four friends did all they could do. They had dreamed about their friend's healing. Their compassion had led them to action and they refused to be defeated by the obstacle the crowd presented. Ultimately, though, there reached a point at which what they could do had ended and what only Jesus could do began. Notice something that's easy to miss in the story:

When Jesus saw their faith
(Mark 2:5)

Jesus saw not the faith of the paralytic but the faith of the friends. I think the Lord still moves in the lives of others because of our faith. That's why we take inventory, team up, take risks, and trust God as we pray.

I believe these Live*Lasters* understood something about responsibility. Responsibility demands compaction. It means that I understand that there is a huge difference between being responsible *for* someone as opposed to being responsible *to* someone.

When I am responsible *for* someone, I expect the person to live up to my expectations.

When I am responsible *to* someone, I accept the person regardless of my expectations.

I trust God even though I can't see the end results or understand what He may be doing in the person's life or my own.

Try naming the five wealthiest people in the world. Name the last five winners of the Miss America competition. Name ten people who have won the Nobel or Pulitzer prizes. Now name four friends who have helped you through a difficult time. Name five people who have taught you something worthwhile. Think of a few people who have made you feel appreciated and special. The people you'll never forget are not the ones with the most credentials, the most money, or the most awards. The people who make a difference in your life are the ones who care. And they will live forever: people who have a little time, a few muscles, a mat, and a lot of love.

I think Mother Teresa was right—we just need to be "a pencil in the hand of God."

Questions for Reflection

1. What's your all-time favorite team and why?

2. If you were going to create a team, who would you choose and what project would you tackle?

3. Where do you see great "compaction" being done?

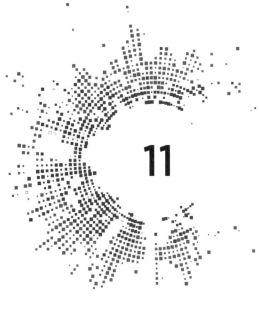

11

Weary

Do you ever need a do-over day? Week? Month?

Every new beginning comes from some other beginning's end.
—Seneca

I've had many of those days, but a memorable one was in Florida when I overslept by setting my alarm clock for 5:30 p.m. instead of 5:30 a.m. Racing to the airport, I remembered I needed gas, but all my stress and strain turned out to be unnecessary when I arrived to find that my flight had been delayed. Once we finally departed, the first leg of my flight was uneventful, but my day got to be more fun on the second flight. The plane was a small one, two seats on each side of the aisle, but I was convinced the space was designed for folks who eat lots of kale and have to jump around in the shower to get wet. I was seated against the window and began praying for a small person to sit next to me or maybe no one at all! The plane appeared to be almost completely loaded, and my neighbor's seat was still empty. I was beginning to think my prayers were being answered when I saw a very big man enter the airplane. Surely he had a seat farther back, I thought, but surely I was wrong. As he plopped into his seat, I found myself pinned to the wall of the aircraft. My new friend seemed completely unaware. I twisted and turned and tried to find a comfortable position for the seventy-five-minute flight ahead, but I wasn't having any success. I thought I would offer a little friendly commentary in case he would take the hint and lean out into the aisle to give me some relief. I suggested that I didn't think these planes were built for guys our size. His response: "Yeah, always my luck to get seated next to the biggest guy on the plane." Now this guy was twice my size, and I decided that might not have been the best thing for me to say. We rode quietly to our next stop, and I stewed about how great my day was going and that this would be a great "do-over" day for me!

I continued feeling bad about my day until I read a story from the *North Bend* (Nebraska) *Eagle* newspaper about the lady who went snow skiing with her husband in Colorado. Apparently her husband talked her into going up the mountain on a day that was comfortable only for polar bears. While they were waiting in the ski-lift line, she realized she was in serious need of a restroom. Someone assured her that there would be one at the top of the lift. After she and her bladder endured a bouncy ride to the top, she discovered that there was no such facility. She began to panic. Her husband suggested that she just go off in the woods and find a nice secluded spot. She was wearing an all-white outfit so she would just blend in with the snow. She didn't have much choice, so she skied past the tree line and arranged her ski suit at half-mast. Fortunately, no one could see her. Unfortunately, her husband hadn't told her to remove her skis. Before you can sing, "Shine on, harvest moon," she was streaking backward across the slope, revealing more about herself than she had ever intended. After all, hindsight is 20/20. With arms flailing and skis sailing, she sped under the very ski lift she had just ridden and collided with a pylon. As she scrambled to recover the essentials, she discovered that her arm was broken. Fortunately, her husband raced to her rescue. He summoned the ski patrol, who transported her to the hospital. While being treated in the emergency room, a man with a broken leg was carried in and placed next to her. By now she had regained her composure enough to make small talk. "So how'd you break your leg?" she asked. "It was the craziest thing you ever saw," he explained. "I was riding up the ski lift and suddenly I couldn't believe my eyes. There was this crazy woman skiing backwards at top speed. I leaned over to get a better look and I guess I didn't realize how far I had moved and fell out of the lift." Then he turned to her and asked, "So how'd you break your arm?"

One of the things I love about the Bible is that there are some "do-over" days revealed. Do you ever read the Bible and think that it's a book that needed a good editor? It seems to me that there are so many stories that shouldn't have been told because they don't make the heroes of the faith look very good. But one of the many things I love about God's Word is that it gives us the good, the bad, and the ugly.

Live*Lasters* understand that there will be some tough days, some days where you would like to take a mulligan, maybe even some weeks or months. What we really need in those moments is not a do-over but a second wind.

There's a character in the Old Testament who found himself in need of a second wind.

Elijah might have been the most exciting, most flamboyant of all the Old Testament prophets. J. Oswald Sanders said this about Elijah:

> **He was like a meteor that flashed across the inky blackness of Israel's spiritual night.**

Elijah's story is brief as he is around for only a few chapters, but it's a wild time (1 Kings 17–19). He shows up and predicts a drought that will last several years and those words made him unpopular, so God told him very specifically, *Get out of town.* Elijah listens and obeys. We then see a great pattern.

- God sends him to a widow with specific instructions to ask for food. Elijah listens and obeys.

- This widow who is preparing the last meal for herself and her son (because they are out of food) obeys Elijah and a miracle happens with the flour pot and the oil jug.

- Then the widow's son dies. Elijah cries out to God for help. God listens and the son is raised from the dead.

- Three years of drought go by and God tells Elijah to go present himself to King Ahab. This was not your ordinary request because Elijah is public enemy number one and on a hit list. But Elijah listens and obeys.

- Now this confrontation leads to a face-off between Elijah and the prophets of Baal, where they have the world's first BBQ cook-off. Elijah prays for fire to light a drenched altar. God listens. People believe. Elijah wins the cook-off.

And then Elijah has a bad day, a day I think he would like to do over.

He runs out into the wilderness and falls asleep. He's exhausted, he's lonely, he feels sorry for himself, he's depressed. God sends an angel with some food and then God asks him a funny question: **What are you doing here?**

Elijah was suffering from something I'm afraid I suffer from often: **spiritual amnesia**

Regardless of how much God has done for me, no matter how many prayers He has answered, blessings He has provided—I'm forgetful and it makes me feel a little better that Elijah was too!

Let me give you a little homework assignment before you lay your head on a pillow tonight. Sit down and make a list of the times that you are absolutely, positively, beyond a shadow of a doubt convinced that God spoke to you, did something for you, intervened, blessed, or made a dramatic difference in a situation. Keep that list handy for spiritual amnesia days!

In 1984 I took a group of teenagers to Costa Rica, where our assignment was to begin the building of a dormitory on the campus of a seminary. Our work was to build the seismic beams, dig the footers, and mix and pour the concrete for the foundation. Now the standard operating procedure on these types of trips is to take before-and-after photos to show the folks back home. We did that. The problem was that you could not tell that we had done anything. All our work was underground. We had worked hard and yet we did not have much to show. The apostle Paul's message from Galatians 6:9 was the verse I found myself quoting then and now, especially on days when I need a second wind:

> **Let us not become weary in doing good,**
> **for at the proper time we will reap a**
> **harvest if we do not give up.**

I read those first few words and think, "Easier said than done!" My assignment, your assignment, the expectation is that we will *be good*, we will *do good*, and we will *keep on* being good and doing good. I get that part, but what I struggle with is the not becoming weary. Who has the right to tell you to do good but not to become weary?

And then I remember who wrote these words. Thirty years had passed since Saul became Paul on the road to Damascus, where he was headed to persecute Christians. Since that time he had preached the good news and was not welcomed in most towns. Persecuted and harassed, he was beaten and left for dead outside the city in Lystra. In Philippi he was severely flogged and thrown into prison (where about midnight he was singing hymns). He was shipwrecked, mocked, and scorned— yet he wrote about not becoming weary.

I confess that I got weary in Costa Rica, and from time to time I get weary where I work in Bethany, Oklahoma. Now when you read Paul's letters you get to thinking that he was a farmer. We know he wasn't, but he used lots of farming illustrations. Sowing and reaping were a favorite of his. In fact, just a verse or two before his challenge to not become weary, he wrote about sowing and reaping. For seven years I lived on a farm of one hundred twenty-two acres. I didn't own any of it but simply enjoyed the big plantation house that sat in the middle of it. I watched the farmer rotate between corn and beans. I saw him walk the fields, inspecting the crop, saying some prayers, and waiting and hoping for a good harvest.

Several years ago I read about the difference between city people and farmers. City people expect and even get angry if not every year is better than the previous year. Farmers know that the coming year may not be as good as the previous year; too many things are unpredictable and beyond their control.

Here is one thing farmers *do* know: **Their only chance at a harvest is to plant, and they will harvest only what they have planted.** Sounds simple, I know, but you would be crazy to plant corn and expect beans!

Paul tells us to plant *good* and *expect better*. I believe that is a key to being a Live*Laster.*

So how do we deal with the inevitable weariness factor that happens when we go around planting good and doing good?

We celebrate what John Wesley talked about often: *the pervasive presence of God.*

I think Jonah's time in the belly of the big fish, Moses' time on the back side of the desert, Paul's time on a ship, and Elijah's time in a cave gave them each a chance to celebrate that pervasive presence of God. It is one of the reasons I want you to create that list. I have mine in my journal. I continue adding to it. I visit it often because I get weary and suffer from spiritual amnesia.

You've heard the expression "He needs a reality check!" I think a nicer way to say it is, "He needs a perspective adjustment!" I got one of those in Haiti when I took a group of university students to the island of La Gonave. We worked in some orphanages and on the construction of a new hospital, which would serve the island's population of 87,000 persons. The construction superintendent told me the story of one of his laborers who requested a day off but was insistent that he could not afford to lose his job. When the superintendent inquired about what was so urgent that he needed to take an unplanned day off, the laborer responded, "I need to bury my children." Apparently two of his children had died during the night from cholera.

One of my favorite phrases is "first world problems." Here are some examples:

- Your iPhone download takes too long.
- Your Starbucks order gets messed up.
- Your flight gets canceled.

An adjusted perspective has a way of changing my weariness and helps me celebrate that even in those moments when it feels that everything that can go wrong has gone wrong, God is there and has something to say, something for me to learn if

I'll simply be still enough long enough so I can experience the pervasive presence of God.

Several years ago Verizon had a series of commercials featuring a man wearing black framed glasses in big cities, swamps, corn fields, and a variety of other places saying these words: "Can you hear me now?" The marketing campaign was both successful and annoying. What you may not know is that at a big NASCAR event, Verizon dressed several hundred men up in black framed glasses with phones to their ears and turned them loose in the crowd as a promotion to find the real "Can You Hear Me Now?" guy.

I wonder sometimes if God, who is speaking to us (and yes, it is a mystery), doesn't feel like screaming, "Can you hear me now?" Live*Lasters* celebrate the pervasive presence of God and are confident that He is always speaking into their lives.

When we find ourselves needing a second wind, we should trust the compass, not the clock, or perhaps a better way of saying this is *Trust the Creator, not the calendar.*

When I get weary, I have typically allowed time to trump direction. What I mean by this is simply that I get impatient. I think things ought to happen faster than they are happening. I want the harvest now. I know some people talk to their plants and maybe their crops too, but I've never seen anything that you can command to grow and it will grow. Unspoken and perhaps somewhat unseen in the law of the harvest is the fact that there is a process. The seed has to die, and in dying there is life. For some period of time you can't see anything growing, and if you tried to see it by digging it up, you would destroy it. You simply wait. Then it pops out of the ground, and unless you have time-lapse photography, you don't see the corn or the beans grow each day, but they do. In the same way I think we need to be reminded that our compass must be set on true north—fixing our eyes on Jesus, the author and perfecter of our faith. We too must die to our own desires and ambitions, humbling ourselves under the mighty hand of God and being confident that we will reap a harvest in due time.

Live*Laster*s understand the importance of knowing where they're going and then simply sticking with it. The Bible says that perseverance develops character and that character develops hope!

When we need a second wind, it is often because we have developed a scarcity mentality and we are too proud to ask for help. Live*Laster*s ask for help.

As a young pastor I reached out to someone I knew only by reputation. He had been a highly successful megachurch pastor and university president. I was delighted when he accepted my invitation to lunch, where I peppered him with questions for several hours. He gave me some advice that I didn't like and I didn't agree with, though I was wise enough not to tell him. As I drove the four hours back home, I thought about what he had told me. His counsel was this: "Keith, your church has everything it needs to be doing everything God expects of it right now. When you need more, He will provide it." I was convinced that he would have a different message if he visited my church. On my return trip I reviewed my mental list of all our church's deficiencies, things that I was convinced would make a difference if we simply had these deficits replaced. For the first three hours and forty-five minutes of my return trip

I was convinced that my solicited mentor was wrong in his judgment, but the closer I got to home the more convinced I became that he was right. We had what we needed for now. We simply were not doing the most we could with what we had been given. So I adjusted my attitude, began giving thanks for what I thought we were missing or didn't have enough of, and God began blessing in ways that I would never have dreamed.

Reaching out to him in a letter felt like a bit of a risk, but his response empowered me and so has continued to do that even to today. If I could give you one important piece of advice it would simply be this: Ask for help! You'll be amazed at who will help you.

When Live*Lasters* want to attack their weariness, they give thanks and ask for advice.

Elijah's experience teaches me one more lesson about second winds. I need to wait on the whisper, the wind, the anointing. On those days that I would like to *do over* when I need a second wind, I simply need to wait.

I am so challenged by these words:

Few things are as hollow as a relationship intended for passion that instead is marked by mere duty.
(Maxie Dunnam)

If ever there was a relationship intended for passion, it's what Christ has called us to as His followers and His servants. But if we're not careful, our ministry becomes a job, our duty, instead of our devotion. I hope you've never been there or are not there now, but again my confession: I have been there.

Years ago I was fishing with a pastor friend who was planting a church. It was not going well. I knew it. He did not know that I knew it. In the middle of the lake he asked me a series of questions:

"Do you ever think about quitting?"

"Yep."

"Why don't you?"

"The *call.*"

"Yep."

That fishing trip turned out to be a second wind for my friend. He returned to his call and continues pursuing it today.

Elijah had one of those special moments on the mountain that day when God asked him, "What are you doing here, Elijah?"

Scripture says there was a powerful wind that tore the mountain apart and shattered the rocks, but the Lord was not in the wind. After the wind there was an earthquake, but the Lord was not in the earthquake. After the earthquake there came a fire, but the Lord was not in the fire. And after the fire came a gentle whisper. Elijah went out and heard the voice of the Lord say, "What are you doing here, Elijah?"

Elijah needed a second wind, a fresh anointing, a chance to regroup, to be refreshed, to be recalibrated.

In my Bible and on my desk I keep a copy of a prayer from John Wesley:

> *Dear Heavenly Father,*
>
> *I am no longer my own, but yours.*
> *Put me to what you will,*
> *place me with whom you will,*

put me to doing,
put me to suffering;
let me be employed for you or set aside by you,
exalted for you or brought low for you;
let me be full, let me be empty;
let me have all things, let me have nothing;
I freely and heartily fully surrender things to your glory
   and service.
And now O wonderful and holy God, Creator, Redeemer
and Sustainer, you are mine and I am yours.
So be it.
And the Covenant which I have made on earth,
   let it also be made in heaven. Amen

I can't imagine a better prayer for those who want to live last!

Questions for Reflection

1. If you could live a day over again, what would it be and how would that day be different?

2. Make a list of the moments in your life when you are certain God intervened, called, or provided.

3. Who in your circle of influence needs some prayer and/or encouragement to begin again or to be reminded of his or her value?

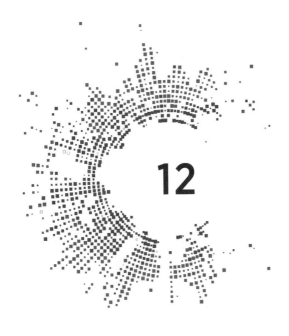

12

More

Are there lessons to learn?

Eventually all things merge into one, and a river runs through it.
—Norman Maclean

"Water always wins" is a favorite expression of a friend of mine. I quoted him often while on vacation in Colorado. I also discovered that there's a big difference between quoting and believing. I was fly-fishing in the Eagle River with my wife and a few friends. The water was high and we knew the river was a little dangerous, so we were being extra careful. While standing in the middle of the river, my friends told me to turn around and look upstream because there was an ice chest headed my way. Apparently someone up the river had lost this cooler and now it was on its way to me. I scooped it up, left my line out in the river, and began walking it to an island in the middle of the river to put it on higher ground where it would be safe. In the midst of my walk to the island, I discovered quite accidentally that I had a fish on my line—my first of the day. An accidental catch but a nice brown trout. After I reeled it in and released it, I went back to fishing and noticed that there were a number of trout coming to the surface just downstream, so I began working my way toward them. The only problem was that with every step I took the water got deeper and the river got stronger.

So my fly-fishing extraordinaire friend was with me fishing in the Eagle River, and this is what he hollered at me—several times:

"Don't go any farther!" I heard him, but then I took one more step—and I now had personal experience as the current grabbed me and carried me several hundred yards down the river.

Note to self: **water always wins!**

After being carried down the river I was able to get to safety. Believe it or not, I had managed to hang on to my fly-rod, my fishing vest, and my hat. I was very wet and I could testify: water always wins!

One of my favorite, perhaps my very favorite Bible story is found in John 21. Here are a few reasons:

1. Fishing—I love to fish! Something about the pursuit of fish, even when you don't catch them, brings me joy.

2. Beach—I love the beach! Some of the moments in life when I feel that God has done some of the toughest work and greatest healing in my life has been while walking along a beach.

3. Breakfast—Doctors say it's the most important meal of the day. I just say it's the best meal of the day. I believe I could eat breakfast for lunch or breakfast for dinner! Call me weird, and many people do, but I love breakfast!

This story from John 21 has all three of these elements. If only it had a golden retriever in the story, it would be the perfect story!

Can you imagine? Fishing all night, as a few of the disciples had done, and catching nothing and then a few words from Jesus and a mega-catch! Breakfast cooked by the King of Kings and the Lord of Lords! (How cool would that be, to say that Jesus cooked breakfast for you?) And then there is a walk on the beach found in this next section of scripture. Listen to these words from John 21:15–23:

> *When they had finished breakfast, Jesus said to Simon Peter, "Simon, son of John, do you love Me more than these?" He said to Him, "Yes, Lord; You know that I love You." He said to him, "Tend My lambs." He said to him again a second time, "Simon, son of John, do you love Me?" He said to Him, "Yes, Lord; You*

know that I love You." He said to him, "Shepherd My sheep." He said to him the third time, "Simon, son of John, do you love Me?" Peter was grieved because He said to him the third time, "Do you love Me?" And he said to Him, "Lord, You know all things; You know that I love You." Jesus said to him, "Tend My sheep.

Truly, truly, I say to you, when you were younger, you used to gird yourself and walk wherever you wished; but when you grow old, you will stretch out your hands and someone else will gird you, and bring you where you do not wish to go." Now this He said, signifying by what kind of death he would glorify God. And when He had spoken this, He said to him, "Follow Me!"

Peter, turning around, saw the disciple whom Jesus loved following them; the one who also had leaned back on His bosom at the supper and said, "Lord, who is the one who betrays You?" So Peter seeing him said to Jesus, "Lord, and what about this man?" Jesus said to him, "If I want him to remain until I come, what is that to you? You follow Me!" (NASB)

I was on what is reported to be this very beach when I made a trip to the Holy Land. Of all the places we visited, this was the highlight of the trip for me. I could see Peter and the disciples out in the boat fishing, I could see Peter jumping in and swimming to shore, I could see Jesus putting His arm around Peter's shoulder and taking him for a walk-and-talk down the beach. As I stood on that beach and thought about

John 21, I was reminded again that Jesus comes *looking* for us! The real-ity is that you can run—but you can't hide from Jesus.

I grew up a few blocks from a beach in Florida. As an adult I had the privilege of living a few blocks from the beach in California. I love beaches and I confess that sometimes I want to live near a beach: East Coast, West Coast, Gulf Coast—it doesn't matter. I would just like to be able to walk on the beach and pray. Simon Peter's walk on the beach with Jesus was one of the most important moments in his life.

When I read or hear someone else's story, I often ask if there are lessons to learn, mistakes to avoid, and truth to hear. Simon Peter's story gives me several challenges:

1. Seven of the disciples went fishing. Verse 3 tells us that they fished all night and **caught nothing**. Now this was not hobby fishing—several of them were "professional" fisherman; in other words, they did this for their livelihood. They were experts. Verse 4 tells us that Jesus, whom they did not recognize, stood on the shore and asked them if they had caught anything. There's nothing worse for a fisherman than not catching fish—unless, perhaps, having someone who's not a fisherman to offer advice, and that's exactly what this man on the shore did. Now if you've been fishing all night and have caught nothing, the last thing you want to do is have to admit it out loud so that everyone can hear. Embarrassing! So this random guy on the shore gave them great advice: *try the other side.* Wow—as if we never would have thought of that! Amazingly, they did

what He said and couldn't even pull the net in because of the amount of fish in it. Now you may be thinking that the real lesson here is *Take Jesus fishing with you* because He is the ultimate fishing guide. And you would be right, but I think the message for LiveLasters is simply this: **go deeper.** If you're not satisfied with your spiritual life, make a commitment that you're going to make changes. You're going to find an accountability partner, you're going to dig deeper into the Word, you're going to pray bigger prayers, you're going to commit to being a part of a small group. You've probably heard the definition of insanity: doing the same thing over and over again and expecting different results. Wherever you find yourself—you can go *deeper* with God, and the ball is in your court.

2. There's a second lesson in this story and one that really resonates with me. It's what I think happened during this walk with Jesus down the beach. I know there's this conversation between Jesus and Peter and there are moments where you think Peter is either really stupid or really hard of hearing because Jesus keeps asking him the same question: **Do you love Me?** In verses 15–17 Jesus asks this same question three times to *one* guy. Now I know and have heard and have preached the sermons about the Greek words for *love* here in this story, but that's not the story in this lesson. For me, when I read this story I think it's simply an invitation to **start over**. Have you ever needed that opportunity on your journey? Simon Peter's problem wasn't the lack of

fish. If you remember the story, he had denied Christ three times, even called down curses in his denials. I'm convinced that the little walk on the beach was all about **restoration**—it was a chance for Peter to be reminded that he was loved and that the call upon his life to *follow* was still in place.

3. The last lesson for me in this story is found in verses 21–22, where Peter gets to looking around and says to Jesus, "What about him?" His reference was to John, a fellow disciple. Peter did what we can all be guilty of doing—he was playing the *comparison game.* We do it in athletics, we do it in the classroom, we do it on the stage, we do it in our families. We have this inclination to look at others and compare ourselves. This wasn't the first time that this had happened in Peter's life, and I think Jesus must have wanted to bury Peter in the sand or baptize him in the Sea of Tiberias—hold him under for only a while until he gained some maturity. But He didn't. He simply reminded Peter that John is not his issue. The message here, I believe, is simply **Follow more closely.** When you're tempted to look at others, that's a good time to pray. When you find yourself thinking about what someone else is getting and you're not, it's a great time to spend more time in the Word. When you're frustrated by the attitudes and actions of others—go sit in front of a mirror for a while. Memorize these words from Hebrews: ***Fix your eyes on Jesus, the Author and Perfector of your faith***** (Hebrews 12:2, author's translation). You've probably seen the bumper

sticker that says, "If you can read this, then you're following too closely." Jesus doesn't have that bumper sticker—you can't follow Him too closely.

Go deeper.
Start over.
Follow more closely.

Live*Lasters* understand that wherever you are with Jesus, there's more; it's never too late to be restored and to start over; following closely to Jesus is always a win.

Questions for Reflection

1. If Jesus were going to ask you the same question three times, what would it be?

2. What's your favorite body of water and why?

3. Have you ever tried to hide from Jesus?

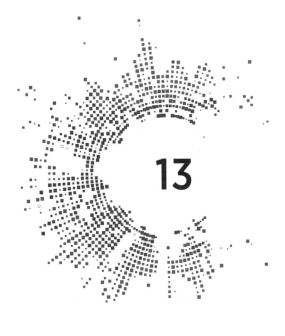

Praise

When was the last time you broke a vase?

Man is born broken. He lives by mending.
The grace of God is glue.
—Eugene O'Neill

From time to time over the years I have invited people to write letters to God. These treasures would become a part of my prayer as I picked them up after worship services. During my prayer time I read the letters to God, something totally unnecessary for Him but beneficial for me. I ask God to help the authors of the letters get the most out of their troubles, not to waste one minute of the pain and hardship they're experiencing, to give them the confidence to say, "God, I can't wait to see what You're going to do with this problem." Nothing written to God has ever surprised Him.

As I read the letters, I'm reminded of a quote I've written in the front of my Bible:

*When you preach, say a good word because
you never know who is out there hanging by their fingertips.*
(Clovis Chappel)

I've tried to follow that advice every time I preach. A little survey to begin this chapter: How many of you love surprises?

Years ago I took a red-eye flight across the country to interview for a job. After a very quick nap in some guest housing being provided by my potential employer, I showered, shaved, and began searching for a comb in my toiletry bag. To my surprise none was to be found. The interview was minutes away and I did not have anything with which to comb my mop of hair. With no transportation, no store within walking distance, and no one to call, panic began setting in. Where is MacGyver when you need him? In my desperation I began combing (no pun intended) this little guest apartment looking for anything that might be used as a comb. With less than two minutes to spare before I was to be picked up for the interview, I saw it: a white plastic fork! It was a cause for celebration on a day when I didn't need that kind of surprise. It also made for a great story when I was introduced a few months later, having been selected for the assignment.

I spent a little time thinking about surprises. The Bible is full of them:

- Adam and Eve stumbling across the grave of Abel
- Noah's neighbors when it began raining
- Sarah telling Abraham that the angel was right
- David with a slingshot knocking out a giant named Goliath
- Jonah's water taxi—a big fish
- Fishermen who worked all night and caught nothing
- Wedding guests at a reception with nothing more to drink than water until . . .
- Ten lepers hanging out together because no one else will hang out with them—and then . . .
- A woman with a history goes to a well at noon to draw some water and learns . . .
- Sitting in a tree to get a good view, Zac is surprised that Jesus knew his name
- The would-be King is celebrated on Palm Sunday, crucified between two thieves on Friday—but then resurrected on Easter Sunday.

I continue to have lots of personal surprises:

- Still surprised by the fact that God loves me
- Even more surprised that God would call me

- Continuing to be surprised that He loves me even though He knows me better than anyone else and wants to be not just my Redeemer—He wants to be my friend.

The fourteenth chapter of Mark tells us the story of a woman who had been surprised by Jesus and did the most surprising thing: **she broke a vase.** Each one of the gospels tells us a similar story of Jesus being anointed with a costly perfume. We're not sure if each story was the same event or if there was more than one time when Jesus had a personal encounter with a Live*Laster,* a servant who accepted a divine demotion and took her place at His feet.

It was only two days before the Passover and the religious community was looking for a way to arrest Jesus and kill Him. Jesus was in Bethany, a city just a mile and a half outside Jerusalem. The exact place was the home of Simon the Leper, not a surprising place for Jesus to be when you recall that He was always interested in the marginal or disposable people of life. This event appears to have pushed Judas over the edge, because immediately following this he went to the chief priests and agreed to betray Jesus to them. Jesus was standing in the shadow of the cross and He knew it. Only a few days remained before He would be arrested and crucified at the site of the town garbage dump outside of Jerusalem. If ever there was a time to *break a vase*, this was it.

You're never quite sure of how history will record a particular event, but you have an idea that some moments in your life are more significant than others. I don't think this unnamed woman knew the significance of what she was doing, but read what Jesus said about it:

> *"Truly I tell you, wherever the gospel is preached*
> *throughout the world, what she has done will also*
> *be told, in memory of her."*
> *(Mark 14:9)*

That prophecy is continuing to be fulfilled and it is happening again today as we consider this story. Here's a personal question: What is the most extravagant expression of love you have ever received? Was there ever a time someone did something for you that you'll never forget? I'm guessing it was not a diamond ring, a fancy car, or a fabulous vacation— all nice things, but they're just that: *things.* Extravagant expressions of love, in my experience, can't be purchased, even with a Mastercard. They're priceless. Here's an even more personal question:

When was the last time you broke a vase?

The Live*Last* message in Mark 14 is all about what can happen if you fall completely and unashamedly in love with Jesus Christ. What we see in this story is something that is not for the casual Christian or the cultural Christian or anyone else interested in the minimum requirements. Those people will never choose to do what this woman chose to do. She offers us a great example if we're interested in living a life that makes a difference. She teaches us that God loves extravagant expressions.

*While he was in Bethany, reclining at the table in
the home of Simon the Leper, a woman [Mark doesn't
even give us her name] came with an alabaster jar of
very expensive perfume, made of pure nard. She broke the
jar and poured the perfume on his head.*
(Mark 14:3)

Think about something. All that perfume surely soaked into Jesus' garments—His robe, His sandals, His outer garment. Surely He bathed and washed, but His outer garments might have retained the aroma for days, maybe an entire week. I wonder if during the course of the coming week there were times in the discouraging moments when the wind blew just right, and He smelled the aroma of the lingering perfume and found encouragement as He remembered this expression of love.

God loves the extravagant. Think about the tabernacle and the temple. These were extravagant houses of worship. There was nothing cheap or "adequate" about these places. It was first class all the way.

Have you read the book of Revelation? Do you see the way the New Jerusalem is described—streets of gold, walls laced with precious stones? A little extravagant, don't you think? God loves it.

The church of early years understood this. In Europe they were not content to erect simple sanctuaries. They built cathedrals! What great places of worship these places are! You walk into one of these houses of worship and feel the sense of awe and the love that provoked such extravagant, impractical, overly expensive places of worship. And God loved it!

And what about that Sistene Chapel? Do you think the people who hired Michelangelo got some criticism? Here they wanted the ceiling painted and it took the guy four years! Why not just use a brush and paint something quaint—nine panels depicting the first chapters of Genesis? And think about it: every day a new section of ceiling would be newly plastered and the artist, using frescos, would have to paint that section before it dried. Is it any surprise that centuries later his work is considered a masterpiece?

I would contend that the key to extravagance is the *condition* or *attention* of the heart. It's possible to be extravagant in a way that all eyes point to you. People say, "What a beautiful church you've built!" or "What a generous gift you've given!" I don't think God loves those kinds of extravagant gifts.

This woman was extravagant in her gift and gave without any reluctance. Quite often our giving is calculated, or maybe I should say *my* giving is calculated. We ask a thousand questions about whether or not we can afford the time to attend that service or make that visit or write that note or give that gift. Sometimes, although we end up doing it, our hearts are not really in it because we're doing it with great reluctance. That is not an extravagant expression of love.

A number of years ago the newspapers were buzzing with a remarkable story. Carlos Rogers of the Toronto Raptors was doing something incredible. He had worked long and hard to make it to the NBA. It was a dream come true. His future, all the benefits he had worked for, were right before him. Now he was possibly throwing it all away. Why? Carlos' sister was sick, very sick. She could not survive without a new kidney. Carlos left his job in the NBA to go home and donate one of his kidneys to his sister. He knew it would end his career—but compared to his love for his sister, he didn't care. *USA Today* called Carlos Rogers the most unselfish man in the NBA. He was living last, serving another, making a gift that was incredibly extravagant but done without reluctance.

Nothing was too precious for the woman to give Jesus. She held nothing as too precious to give to Him. And what she gave was worth more than one year's wages.

Consider how much that is. To really get a feel for it, you have to translate it into today's economy. Consider for a moment how much you make in a year. What is your gross salary and benefits? What is your total package for an entire year? Now add approximately three more months to that, because what she offered was worth over three hundred days of work. There are only two hundred sixty weekdays in an average year. That includes the time we take for vacation. For you to give what she gave, you would have to give the figure you now hold in your mind. But that is precisely what she gave.

And I'm sure what she gave cost her. There is no indication that she was wealthy. What she gave cost her, just as if you gave a year's wages it would cost you. That's a mark of extravagant love. That's a mark of genuine Christian giving.

When he wanted to make a sacrifice to God, David approached a Jebusite. He wanted to buy his threshing floor so he could build an altar and make a sacrifice to God. The man wanted to give David everything he needed—the threshing floor, the wood for the altar, and the oxen for the sacrifice. But David would not accept it. He told him that he wanted to buy it for a price, adding, **"I will not sacrifice to the Lord my God burnt offerings that cost me nothing"** (2 Samuel 24:24). David recognized, and we should too, that for an offering to be meaningful, it must cost us something.

But even though it cost this woman a great deal, she rejoiced in the fact that she had been given the privilege to give it. It wasn't a burdensome gift. It was a gift of love. It was a gift that was an example of love's extravagance.

One of my great concerns today is that we live in a time of minimum requirements. Maybe it has always been that way, but it seems as though we want to know what is the least we can get by with. I would love to see a return to what was once known as the Protestant work ethic. I love people who go the second and third mile, and I get frustrated with people who want to do whatever the minimum is.

As a graduate student, I had a professor who told a story about a lesson he learned early in his teaching career. His detailed syllabus allowed students to determine how many points they needed to earn to pass and what it would take to achieve each letter grade. Two of the students in this class did very well, attended all of the classes in the initial weeks, and scored high on the examinations—and then they disappeared. The professor became concerned about them and went looking for them. When he caught up with them, he inquired to see if everything was okay. They assured him that things were fine. When he asked why they were no longer attending class, they told him that by their calculations they had earned enough points to pass the class and that was all they were looking for.

They simply wanted to meet the minimum standard, nothing less and nothing more.

Nothing I read in Scripture supports this idea of minimum requirements. God loves extravagant expressions of love, and because He is not here on earth in the flesh, I believe He wants us to demonstrate our love for Him with extravagant expressions of love for each other. So let me ask again—**When was the last time you broke a vase?**

This story reminds me that opportunity doesn't always knock twice.

> *"Leave her alone," said Jesus. "Why are you bothering her?*
> *She has done a beautiful thing to me. The poor you will*
> *always have with you, and you can help them any time*
> *you want. But you will not always have me."*
> *(Mark 14:6–7)*

There are some things that have to be done at that particular moment or they can never be done again. Anointing Jesus in the shadow of the cross was one of those moments that needed to be seized.

There was apparently no intention of spreading out the use of this expensive perfume, so she broke the neck of the flask and proceeded to pour the entire contents on Jesus. It appears that she started with His head and let the liquid run down on the rest of His body, ending up at His feet.

It's hard for us to really comprehend the significance of what she did. I love to buy my wife perfume. I've been doing that since before we were married. I think the perfume I purchase for her is expensive, but I've never considered it extravagant. It does not cost me three hundred days' wages.

We might do well to put this whole matter of "extravagance" into its proper perspective. When King Ahasuerus was searching for a new queen to replace Vashti, the women who were chosen as candidates went through a rather *extravagant* preparation process:

> *Each young woman's turn came to go in to*
> *King Ahasuerus after she had completed twelve months'*
> *preparation, according to the regulations for the women,*
> *for thus were the days of their preparation apportioned: six*
> *months with oil of myrrh, and six months with perfumes*
> *and preparations for beautifying women.*
> (Esther 2:12 NKJV)

Do something good and there's almost always a result on which you can count—someone will criticize you. This is especially true whenever someone does something extravagant—there will be critics. This was no exception. There were two primary criticisms:

First, the critics said, "What a waste!" Can't you hear them? A lesser perfume would have been just as effective. Or—less of the perfume would have been just as effective. But would it?

Second, the critics said, "How irresponsible!" This is the guilt response. The thought is that if the perfume had been sold and the money given to the poor, so much more good could have been accomplished.

Jesus also told these critics, "The poor you always have with you—but I am here only a little while." Now Jesus is not telling us to disregard the poor. He is not telling us to live self-indulgently. Jesus is telling us to make the most of the opportunities that come our way. When you have a chance to show love in an extravagant way—**break a vase**!

For many of us the most extravagant thing we could do would have nothing to do with money and everything to do with our time because time is what we have the least amount of. For others it would be doing something else, but remember: when you do something really extravagant, the chances are good that you'll be criticized. Just check the attention of your heart: is your extravagance flowing out of self-abandonment, a decision to live in the present, to choose not to listen to the crowd?

I can't make you express your love for God in an extravagant way. The truth is that it wouldn't be something extravagant if I could do that. All I can do is remind you that Live*Lasters* understand the value of breaking a vase. And that brings us to one more thought: some gifts are always remembered. That's true in your life and true in mine. Jesus said,

> *"She did what she could. She poured perfume*
> *on my body beforehand to prepare for burial."*
> *(Mark 14:8)*

The first five words of that verse slapped me in the face: **She did what she could**. This story teaches us a simple but profound truth: **She gave what she *had*.**

I think we often have the idea that we are going to wait until we get something before we give something extravagant to

God. Instead, God chooses to use simple things like sack lunches and empty jars to do things that are always remembered.

When I was fifteen years old I attended a denominational church conference in Miami. I was a kid from a single-parent family that had worked to earn barely enough money to be there. My best friend was a couple of years older and we had traveled together. I'll never forget seeing one of the senior citizens from our church. Her name was Velma. She was a widow. I did not know her well. She greeted me and we talked briefly. Then she reached out and shook my hand. I felt something in it. As she walked away I saw that it was a five-dollar bill. It was significant and extravagant. Now fast-forward ten years and I was a young Houston police officer serving as a volunteer youth pastor in my home church. One afternoon I was walking through the old sanctuary (now the youth center) and it was dark. I could hear a voice. I stopped and listened. It was Velma, ten years older now, a senior citizen. She was kneeling at an altar praying (something that I learned later was her regular practice in this room). She had no idea that I was walking through during her prayer. But as I listened I heard my name—I heard her praying for me. She was *breaking a vase!*

Can you think of a time when someone did something special that he or she didn't have to do, was not expected to do? If you've had that wonderful experience you won't ever forget it. Maybe the person—

- traveled way out of his or her way
- stayed the night with you in a quiet hospital room

- gave you a gift that touched you to the core of your being

- met a need that seemed impossible

- made it possible for you to do something you've always wanted to do

- listened to you when that was all you needed— someone to listen

The frequent expressions of love are like oxygen to us—we need them. But those extraordinary acts of love—we return to them again and again and enjoy their sweet aroma over and over.

When was the last time you "broke a vase"? When was the last time you did something for someone that was not the sensible, safe thing to do?

Most importantly, have you ever done something extravagant out of your love for the Lord? Have you ever let yourself go and "broken a vase," spurning the naysayers, focusing only on the Lord? Have you ever thrown caution to the wind and let love for the Savior guide your heart?

There's something kind of melancholy about sitting around a campfire and watching it go out. Those dying embers are destined to become cold ashes if left alone. The same thing can happen in a relationship. What Christ wants more than anything else with us is a relationship. It's not about ritual; it's not about religion. Think about the relationships in your life**. What do extravagant expressions of love do for your relationships?** I'm guessing they create a new spark, rekindle the fire, keep you from watching dying embers go out.

What would happen in your relationship with Christ if you took to heart the kind of example set for us in Mark 14?

I don't know where that kind of love might lead us. I don't know what opportunities may be available to you. I don't know how I might be able to love Him extravagantly. But then, if we knew what we were "supposed" to do, it wouldn't be extravagant. It wouldn't be the kind of love that creates an aroma that brings delight even in the worst of circumstances.

Look for an opportunity. Keep your eyes wide open. And when you find that opportunity—**break a vase**!

Back in 1988 Orel Hershiser was the best pitcher in baseball. Following the World Series he was invited to be a guest on a late-night television talk show. The hilarious host asked Hershiser about something everyone had seen on national television during the World Series. In the dugout between innings, sometimes it appeared that he was singing to himself. The host asked him what he was singing. Hershiser told him he was singing the doxology. The host did not know what that was and asked him if he would sing it. And he did.

It was a *break a vase* moment.

Questions for Reflection

1. What is the most extravagant gift you have ever given?

2. Who needs you to break a vase for him or her?

3. Can you write a letter to God and then read it to Him out loud?

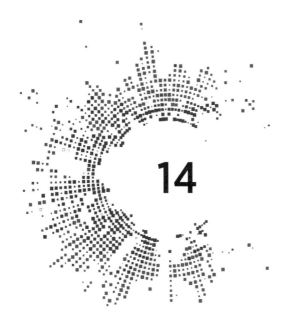

Images

***Are you building something that will last, has purpose,
and will make a difference?***

A different world cannot be built by indifferent people.
—Peter Marshall

I like **stories** better than **sermons**. I like **pictures** better than **words**.

Jesus painted word pictures and told stories when He spoke.

One of my favorites comes at the conclusion of what is commonly called the Sermon on the Mount. For three chapters Jesus has given us instructions about how to be happy, what we can do to make a difference in life, things we should do and things we should not do, how to pray, where our focus should be. He uses wonderful images of salt and light, lilies and lamps, moths and money, birds and barns, pearls and pigs, snakes and fish, planks and gates, wolves and sheep, and then He concludes this sermon with one last story:

> *"Therefore, everyone who hears these words of*
> *mine and puts them into practice is like a wise man who*
> *built his house on the rock. The rain came down,*
> *the streams rose, and the winds blew and beat against*
> *that house; yet it did not fall because it had its foundation*
> *on the rock. But everyone who hears these words of mine*
> *and does not put them into practice is like a foolish man*
> *who built his house on sand. The rain came down,*
> *the streams rose, and the winds blew and beat against that*
> *house, and it fell with a great crash."*
> *(Matthew 7:24–27)*

On a long flight from Dallas, Texas, to Brisbane, Australia, I found myself in conversation with my seatmate, who was traveling to visit family. The purpose of my trip was business with one day set aside for tourism. My new friend asked me how I was going to spend that day. When I told him that I didn't know and asked him for advice, he suggested that I climb the Sydney Harbour Bridge. This was an activity I had never considered and didn't know was possible. Though my fellow traveler had never climbed the bridge, he had heard that it was fun, though a little bit expensive, and encouraged me to give it a try. I thanked him and never thought about it again until I found myself at a cookout a few nights later in Sydney. My host and I were getting to know each other while he manned the grill and he asked me what I was going to do on my one day to see the sights in Sydney. Once again I told him that I didn't know and asked for suggestions. He quickly recommended that I climb the Sydney Harbour Bridge. When I shared with him my conversation from the plane ride, he concluded that this adventure must be calling me. I asked if he had ever climbed the bridge and learned that he had not as it was a little too expensive for him, but he had friends who had completed the climb and they highly recommended it. Once again, I tucked the idea away and doubted that this would be how I would spend my one day of fun in Australia. But then I found myself in downtown Sydney having lunch in a rotating restaurant looking out over this magnificent city. Across the table from me was a very successful businessman, and the purpose of our lunch was a potential partnership between an organization where he volunteered his time and the university where I was employed. As the restaurant rotated and the famed Sydney Opera House and Sydney Harbour Bridge came into clear view, I casually mentioned that I had recently learned that you could climb the Sydney Harbour Bridge. Imagine my surprise when my new friend stated, "I own that. Would you like to make the climb?" "You own the bridge?" "No, not the bridge, but the climbing service." Wow! Now I was beginning to believe that I really was supposed to climb this beautiful structure, which had been built in the 1920s and early 1930s. So the next day I climbed the Sydney Harbour Bridge, a wonderful experience that I highly recommend.

This crazy story led me to want to know more about the building of the bridge (an idea that was conceived a century before construction started) and the vision to create a span that originally served hundreds of vehicles each week and now handles hundreds of thousands of vehicles per day. The bridge was built bigger and stronger for much more than the original need and took longer and was more expensive than initial conceptions—and I am guessing there were naysayers along the way. One little side note: the objections to the climbing service for this massive bridge were so numerous that it took my friend and his brother more years to overcome these obstacles and gain approval for their business than it had to build the bridge! I learned something about perspective and perseverance from my Sydney Harbour Bridge experience.

You and I are in the building business. Every single day we are involved in construction or demolition or renovation.

In the movie *Gladiator* there's a line I love:

What we do in life echoes in eternity.
(Maximus)

Have you spent much time thinking about your echo? I wonder if often we're completely unaware of the message we're sending to those who are listening and watching. It is possible, I believe, to have an echo that would make us cringe if we only knew how it was being received.

Bubba Smith was a professional football player who experienced the ache of the echo when he returned to his alma mater, Michigan State University, for homecoming activities. At the time, he was a highly paid commercial spokesperson for a popular beer. The company's advertising campaign featured a catchy slogan: "tastes great—less filling." The homecoming parade crowd, filled with students on both sides of the street, saw Bubba and began shouting the slogan in an unrehearsed response: " Tastes great—less filling!"

Bubba Smith decided that day that he did not like that echo and stepped away from his lucrative contract as the company spokesperson.

A number of years ago I was in Scottsville, Texas, population 283, to speak at a youth camp. Located immediately adjacent to the campground is one of the oldest and most historic cemeteries in the state of Texas. One morning I decided to walk through the cemetery. Many of the grave markers show birth dates in the 1700s. One of the large monuments recognizes the death of a soldier who fought in the Battle of 1812. The inscription on his monument said, "O for the touch of a vanish'd hand, And the sound of a voice that is still!"

One of the things you find in old cemeteries that's different from more recent ones is the inscriptions on the tombstones. Today you see the name, date of birth, and date of death, maybe a Scripture verse. But in years gone by the stones were marked with all kind of prose, some of it a bit humorous, some you're not quite sure how to take, and some thought-stirring and soul-provoking. I was glad I had a pencil in my pocket and a piece of paper with me so I could write down some of the things I read:

On one man's grave were these words: "Wise enough to marry a Texan!"

On the grave of an eighteen-year-old: "As you are now, so once was I. As I am now, so you must be. Prepare for death and follow me."

I really liked this one: "Life's race well run. Life's work well done. Life's crown well won. Now comes rest."

Cemeteries are great places to make big decisions. Spend some time in a cemetery as you think about the future, and you will quickly be reminded that life on earth is finite; it is temporal. You need to make decisions, especially the most significant decisions in light of eternity—and a cemetery is a good place to do that.

I can't take you to a cemetery, but I can point you to Scripture. Jesus tells us in the Sermon on the Mount that we need to—

- Pursue happiness by having the right attitude (Matthew 5:1–12)

- Live in such a way that others will see our good deeds and celebrate God (5:13–16)

- Be ambassadors of reconciliation (5:17–26)

- Practice sexual purity (5:27–30)

- Marry for a lifetime (5:31–32)

- Keep your promises (5:33–37)

- Go the second mile in all you do (5:38–42)

- Love your enemies (5:43–46)

- Give generously (6:1–4)

- Pray big (6:5–14)

- Fast quietly (6:16–18)

- Remember where you will spend eternity (6:19–24)

- Don't worry—get your priorities in order (6:25–34)

- Don't judge because that's not your job (7:1–6)

- Make the Golden Rule come alive for others (7:7–12)

- Choose your path of travel carefully (7:13–14)

- Be careful who you spend time with (7:15–23)

- And finally, *build wisely* (7:24–27)

Take a survey of people over the age of fifty, and one of the things I believe you will hear is that **they did not start thinking soon enough about what they were building**. In other words, life was simply happening, they were having fun, making decisions, dealing with what life sent their way—and suddenly they woke up and realized that they had built a life but were not that excited about the echo in eternity.

Tony Campolo tells a great story about graduation Sunday in the church where he was worshiping. The graduates were marched into church with great pomp and circumstance and seated on the first few rows. These youngsters were dressed in their robes and mortarboards and the message that day was directed specifically toward them with their families and friends in the audience allowed to listen in. The pastor began his sermon with a painful but powerful message. He told these graduates that they were going to die. While very true, it is not exactly the message anyone is seeking to hear in the prime of his or her life. He went on to tell them that after they died, then their bodies would be placed in the ground, dirt would be thrown onto their caskets, and then everyone would go back to the church and eat potato salad and talk about them. Among the questions the pastor asked on that day was simply this:

Will you have a title or will you have a testimony?

Campolo's pastor was direct and he was right. Titles don't matter much on our day of death, but testimonies are precious. So here's my advice to you about how to have a Live*Last* testimony on that day when folks gather at the church to eat potato salad and talk about you.

- **Read** scripture. But I warn you that when you read scripture it will change your life. Untold thousands of people who have come and gone before us would testify that God's Word jumped off the page and changed their destiny forever. Don't believe me—try a little experiment. For seven days read from your Bible each and every day until you believe God speaks to you. Some days you might read several chapters before He speaks and other days it will be in the very first verse. Keep a record. Write down what you hear, what you feel, what you sense God's Word is saying to you.

- **Soak** in scripture. This is a deeper dive. Maybe it's a day away with just your Bible, pen, and your journal, or maybe it's joining a small group with a commitment to studying a particular passage or book of the Bible. It might even be something a bit radical like spending a month or even a year reading the same chapter every single day, looking and listening for what the Holy Spirit wants to teach you. Here's what I know: **If you're going to live in the world successfully, I believe you need to live in the Word consistently.**

- **Pray** scripture. Try this. I dare you. Pick a passage and begin to pray those verses each day. Praying scripture is another discipline that can change your life and give you a testimony for that potato-salad-eating day. (Psalm 23, Romans 8, and Ephesians 4 are good places to start.)

- **Memorize** scripture. There are lots of promises in God's Word for those who make memorization a priority in their lives. Start with one verse and add a verse a week or even a verse a month. Any amount of memorized scripture will guarantee to make a difference in your life. I don't know of anyone who has changed the world for Christ who did not make God's Word a focus in his or her life.

- **Live** scripture and let scripture **live in** you. Do it quietly, do it humbly, do it consistently. If you were to ask me to name my most important material possession, it would be an easy answer: my mom's Bible. Though her death was a surprise to the family, she had made preparations. We all knew that heaven would be her home. She had made it clear for years by her words and her actions that she was a child of the King and that she was confident about her destination. She had also prepared a Bible for each of her children and grandchildren. These Bibles were not new ones—they were Bibles she had used. Each one featured her personal notes, underlined passages, and special messages to us. As the eldest child I was privileged to receive her most-used Bible.

She left behind very little in regard to things of earthly value. She possessed no college degrees, professional certifications, or fancy titles. Her potato-salad day was standing-room-only though, and throughout that crowd were people who had benefited from the influence and impact of her life. They gave testimony to the difference she had made for them.

I have one last story. Remember: I like stories better than sermons. It's about my mom, it's about scripture, and it's about a day when I got a new title. On the morning of my inauguration as president of Southern Nazarene University, I arrived early to my office for some last-minute preparations on the message I would deliver in just a few hours. I was reflecting on a dinner we had hosted in our home the night before and the scripture I was planning to focus on in my inaugural address.

> *Sitting down, Jesus called the Twelve and said,*
> *"Anyone who wants to be first must be the very last,*
> *and the servant of all."*
> *(Mark 9:35)*

Friends and family had told me repeatedly the same message the night before—they wished my mom could have been here to see this day when her son was inaugurated as a university president. They knew she would be very proud. I knew they were right, and though she had been gone for many years, my mother continued as a great champion and cheerleader in my life.

So, standing in my office thinking about my mom and Mark 9:35, I decided to pull her Bible off my shelf and see if she had any notes connected to this verse. Her Bible, like many, featured two columns per page, and this particular verse started at the bottom of the page in the first column. I was not surprised to see that she had underlined the verse. As I read the verse and my eyes moved to the top of the second column, I was surprised to see a line running from the end of the verse back to the top left corner of the page. There in the corner were these words printed in my mom's distinctive writing: "Keith, this is what real success is." One more time, seventeen years after her passing, she was sending me a message through scripture and her testimony. Her echo continues!

Questions for Reflection

1. How do you feel about what you're building?

2. Do you like the echo for eternity?

3. Who could help you know what your echo really sounds like? (someone who would tell you the hard truth and help you understand the message your words and actions are communicating)

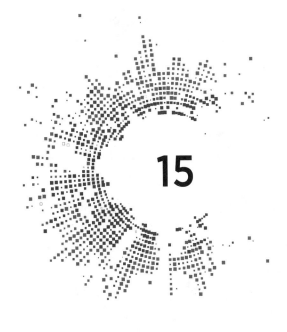

Mercy

Do you have any doubts along the way?

Doubt isn't the opposite of faith; it is an element of faith.
—Paul Tillich

Do you have any doubts along the way? Do you ever wonder if there really is a God, and, if there is a God, what He's doing—in your life, in the lives of others? Do you ever think that He might love your brother or sister or roommate or friend more than you? Does He care about the injustice and inequity in the world—in your world?

If you answered yes to any of the questions above, then you're in great company. Doubt is a reality for us all and an opportunity for us to strengthen and deepen our faith. Spend some time in God's Word and you'll see the phrase "the way" or "the path" used often. I've been reading, listening, and trying to understand all I can about the way of God. Early Christians were known as "people of the Way." Choosing to live last means that you're going to follow the way or path that God has described, and if your experience is anything like that of the millions who have gone before you, there will be some doubts along the way.

I watched a segment of a morning news show recently that left me kind of bummed. It suggested that children being born today may never own a car. Mass transit, ride sharing—the commentators had a whole list of reasons that kids born today might not ever know the joy of a first car. Now that may not bother you, but I admit that the thought of not owning a car was depressing to me. My first car wasn't very attractive, but it had four wheels and an engine, and it was mine. I remember installing a special sound system including an eight-track tape player, something that some of you reading this book have never heard of. Dinosaurs weren't walking the earth at this time, but this was still a long time ago! Over the years I've loved owning a variety of cars. I once had a 1966 Ford Mustang, a 1954 Ford pickup, and I even owned a Corvette. My wife tells people that the biggest reason she wanted to go out with me was because of my Corvette. She wanted to drive it. I never knew that until years after we were married. Strangely enough, I never let her drive it.

Before I could get a driver's license I had to take a driver's education course after school and then had to take the written examination. I still remember trying to learn how many feet it took to stop a car at certain speed limits. At the time I thought, "Boy, are these stupid things to learn! If you're going fifty-five miles per hour and you have to stop suddenly, who has time or the desire to count the feet it takes to stop?" Most of us have seen the bumper sticker that says, "If you can read this, you're too close!" And maybe you've seen the message on the back of eighteen-wheelers that says, "If you can't see my mirrors, I can't see you!" I found out as a young police officer that there was a very good reason for learning those stopping distance statistics. One of my least favorite responsibilities as a police officer was the investigation of automobile accidents. I once was sent to the scene of a twelve-car pile-up. One car slowed down and the eleven drivers behind him couldn't stop in time. The problem in that situation is that every driver who struck the car in front of him or her was responsible for the damage. You see, the law says you can't follow too closely.

When my son was learning to drive we told him over and over and over again that he needed to slow down and keep enough distance between his car and the one in front of him. Regrettably, he didn't listen—and about six weeks after we bought his first car, we got a call that he had hit the car in front of him at a traffic light. Fortunately, no one was hurt, but it was an expensive lesson as his car was totaled. It's amazing what we can learn from experience, especially the painful moments in life.

Jesus had His disciples on a crash course of education. He would spend only a few years with them, and then He was depending on them to establish the church and carry out the mission of taking the gospel to every living creature, a mission that continues today. It's a Live*Last* mission. The disciples were in basic training and never does that seem to be as evident as is seen in Matthew 14:22–33, the story of Jesus walking on the water and then inviting Peter to join Him. In order to really appreciate this story, we need a little more context for what's going on in this training. Two things have just happened:

1. Jesus gets word that His cousin, John the Baptist, has been executed by beheading.

2. Jesus feeds five thousand men, plus women and children.

So you have some horrible news followed by a big-time miracle. Can you imagine what would have happened on Twitter and Facebook if this many people were fed with only five loaves of bread and two fish supplied by a little boy?

Following this amazing miracle, Matthew uses a couple of interesting words to describe what Jesus did next. Verse 22 uses the word *immediately.* I say it's interesting because this word would more likely be used in Mark's gospel. Mark was a young man in a hurry. Matthew was much more precise. He had an accountant's mind-set, but he chose the word *immediately* to describe the action that Jesus took following the miracle. The second interesting word to me is *made,* also in verse 22. Matthew tells us that Jesus *made*—or another translation could be *forced* or *compelled* the disciples to get into the boat and go without Him to the other side while He dismissed the crowd. Seems like a really strange thing that Jesus forced or compelled or made the disciples do. Why in the world wouldn't He want some help dismissing the crowd? Why wouldn't He want his disciples to go with Him when he went up on the mountain to pray? Why would He put them in harm's way by sending them out in a boat if He knew the wind and the waves were going to be dangerous?

Was this an accident, a random coincidence—or was there something else to be learned?

Several years ago I was at the breakfast table reading *Jesus Calling*, by Sarah Young. I read these words: **Trust God with every detail of your life. Nothing is random in His kingdom.**

I confess to you that I still wrestle with those words: *every detail. Nothing is random.*

At the age of twelve I was the oldest male in my family. No grandfathers, no uncles, no cousins, and no father actively engaged in my life. Through a series of tragedies and poor choices, the male population of my family disappeared.

While I believed what Jesus said, *I am the Way, the Truth, and the Life*, I had entered this season of adolescence with a great deal of doubt. Why me? This isn't fair. I hadn't done anything to deserve this.

Here's what I discovered during that season:

> **When our experience doesn't match our expectation, a gap is created. In that gap are disappointment and doubt.**

So here's my question for you: What do you do with your doubts?

Start by counting the cost. That's exactly what a Live*Last* lifestyle requires. John the Baptist was a Live*Last* leader, and when I think about doubts I think about this cousin of Jesus. He preached a message of repentance. Large crowds followed him. He baptized Jesus. He had a significant ministry until he stepped over the line because he stood for a little too much righteousness. His problems began when he called the king on the carpet. On a trip to Rome King Herod fell in lust with his brother's wife. So, he divorced his wife and brought his sister-in-law home. While others gossiped, John the Baptist called it just what it was: *adultery.* His new wife didn't like what he was saying, so she convinced Herod to have John the Baptist thrown in jail. Now Jesus was still around at this time, and since He had the power to give sight to the blind, walk on water, feed five thousand—getting John out of jail shouldn't have been a big deal. But He didn't. Then things got worse. King Herod in a drunken moment promised anything to the dancing daughter of his new mistress. After conferring with her mother, she announced that she wanted John the Baptizer's head on a platter. That kind of persecution is a little more than people insulting you and saying evil things about you. There's not much fair in this story.

Even before the death sentence had been handed down, John the Baptist had begun having some doubts. He sent one of his disciples to Jesus with this question:

> *"Are you the one who is to come,*
> *or should we expect someone else?"*
> *(Matthew 11:3)*

John was human. He was struggling with the fact that Jesus hadn't done anything to relieve the persecution he was experiencing. Jesus hadn't even been to visit him in jail. God had the power to do something, but it appeared that He was sitting on His hands.

Jesus got John's message, and His reply is interesting for several reasons. First, He didn't get mad. He didn't sit down and write a long letter detailing all that He had experienced or was about to experience. Jesus demonstrates to us again that God never turns away the questions of someone who is sincerely searching for answers.

Jesus replied, "Go back and report to John what you hear and see: The blind receive sight, the lame walk, those who have leprosy are cleansed, the deaf hear, the dead are raised, and the good news is proclaimed to the poor. Blessed is anyone who does not stumble on account of me."
(Matthew 11:4–6)

Jesus' words were the words of the prophet Isaiah referring to the coming Messiah. Another way you could say it is this: *Tell John that everything is going as planned.* There is no fine print in Scripture; Jesus makes it clear that there is a cost to following Him. But He invites us on a journey that will not be without moments of doubt along the way.

Live*Lasters* learn to follow closely and follow directions. Unlike driving a car, where it is very possible to follow too closely, Jesus invites us to get close. I love what a friend of mine often says: **Wherever you are with God, there is more for you.** I believe that. I've experienced that. We follow closely when we spend time in His Word and in the spiritual disciplines. Now that doesn't mean that you won't have moments of doubt. The disciples were living with Jesus and still had moments of doubt. But your expectations and your experience will be more in line when you soak yourself in God's Word.

Live*Lasters* look for God in the storm. I'm convinced that this experience in Matthew 14 was a part of the curriculum for the disciples. Though they did not get a printed syllabus that told them what was going to happen when they got into the boat to go ahead of Jesus, I believe He wanted them to experience an actual storm and see Him walking on the water. I also believe with all my heart that Jesus has used the storms in my life to educate and grow me in my faith, especially if I look for Him and trust Him in the storms *and* on the sunny days. Now I don't believe our Father looks down from heaven each morning and says, "I wonder who I can mess with today! Who needs a flat tire or a failing grade? Who needs to go through cancer or a car wreck?" I don't believe life works like that. I do believe He knows who is looking for help and for Him in the storm.

Stepping out in faith is another important step for those who choose to live last. Several years ago I traveled with my daughter and a group to the Holy Land. One of the experiences we enjoyed together was a boat trip on the Sea of Galilee. It was daylight, it was calm, we had life jackets, I could see the shore, and I can swim. It did not take any faith for me to step into that boat and sail with that group. But almost thirty years ago I was fishing from a boat in northern Arkansas. We were on what is called a "heat" lake. These are lakes connected to power plants. The power plants circulate the water from the lake through their facility and then return it to the lake at a warm eighty-five degrees. Fish love it and they grow big, fast. Fishermen love to fish in heat lakes. I was one of those fishermen, at least until the time I was fishing at 3:00 a.m. and a cold front hit the lake with 40 mph winds and freezing precipitation. The warm water, mixed with the sleet and snow, created fog. I can honestly say that I was fearful for my life. I truly did not think we would make it off the lake. Obviously I did, but that experience gave me a whole new appreciation for what Peter did that night when he stepped out of the boat and walked toward Jesus. Peter did what no one else did sometime between 3:00 and 6:00 a.m. when he stepped out of the boat and walked toward Jesus. When you find yourself in times of doubt, you will either walk toward Jesus or away from Him. And sometimes it's really hard to take your first step of faith—especially when everyone else in the boat is remaining seated.

Here's some extremely practical advice on how to deal with doubts.

Remember what He has done in the past.

Keep a journal of how God has helped you in the past. It seems to me that we all have moments of what I referred to previously in the book as spiritual amnesia, but a journal helps us remember how God provided, or healed, or stepped in and rescued us in days gone by. Another great thing to remember are some of the great doubters from days gone by; people like—

- Abraham

- Moses

- Gideon

- David (By the way his journals are much of what we see in the Psalms. Read the Psalms and you'll discover that there were moments of great anguish, some anger, and lots of transparency—exactly what a great journal should feature).

- Jonah

- All of the disciples, but especially a guy named Thomas. He is often referred to as "doubting Thomas," but his story greatly encourages me. Jesus knew Thomas needed to see and to touch, and He let him. Legend has it that Thomas served as a missionary in India, where he died as a result of a spear wound to his side. Though we don't know whether the legend is true, how ironic would it be that Thomas, the one who touched the wounds in the side of Jesus, would himself die as a result of this kind of wound?

Here's another reminder of what it means to model a LiveLast lifestyle.

Have mercy on those who doubt.

Do you remember these words from the short book of Jude?

Keep yourselves in the love of God as you wait for the mercy of our Lord Jesus Christ to bring you to eternal life. Be merciful to those who doubt. (Jude 21–22)

It's interesting to me that we find this verse in this tiny book. The theme of Jude is false teaching or apostasy. It's a bold little book written to believers about the importance of the faith and sound doctrine. Jude calls on the church to contend for the faith. In this fiery little book tucked away in its twenty-five short verses is the instruction to have mercy on those who doubt. Why? Because every single one of us will have doubts along the way.

Right now I have some people in my life who are doubting. One has so many doubts that he now describes himself as a "Christian atheist"—Christian by culture, atheist by belief. Others I know are wrestling with where God is and what He's doing in their lives—some painful moments, some moments along the way that can be lonely.

The disciples in the boat that night were on a journey with Jesus. I'm convinced their experiences with Him were all about growth—taking that seed of faith that had led each of them to answer His invitation to follow—and watering and feeding so that there would be a harvest in the days ahead, a harvest that would lead to the establishment of the church that continues today. This boat experience recorded in Matthew 14 was not the first time they had seen Jesus deal with the wind and the water. Six chapters back, in Matthew 8, you might remember that the whole team was in another boat—only this time Jesus was asleep. Matthew tells us that a furious storm came up on the lake so that the waves swept over the boat. But Jesus was sleeping. They woke Him up, convinced that they were going to drown. He spoke these words: *You of little faith, why are you so afraid?* Then He spoke to the wind and the waves, and Scripture tells us it became completely calm. The end of that lesson is found in Matthew 8:27:

The men were amazed and asked,
"What kind of man is this?
Even the winds and the waves obey him!"

Fast-forward now to Matthew 14 and see the progression in the journey of the disciples as we read the end of the lesson:

And when they climbed into the boat,
the wind died down. Then those who were in the boat
worshiped him, saying, "Truly you are the Son of God."
(Matthew 14:32–33)

Earlier in this chapter I referenced some words from *Jesus Calling*, by Sarah Young. Let me close this chapter with another paragraph from this same book. I hope you will read, reflect, and meditate upon her thoughts about the message Jesus might have for each of us as we travel His path.

YOU'RE ON THE RIGHT PATH. Listen more to Me and less to your doubts. I am leading you along the way I designed just for you. Therefore, it is a lonely way, humanly speaking. But I go before you as well as alongside you, so you are never alone. Do not expect anyone to understand fully My ways with you, any more than you can comprehend My dealings with others. I am revealing to you the path of Life, day by day and moment by moment. As I said to My disciple Peter, so I repeat to you: **Follow Me.**

Questions for Reflection

1. Make a list of any doubts that might be troubling you at this moment in your life. Now speak them out loud in prayer, admitting them to God and to yourself.

2. Which of the Bible's "doubters" do you most identify with? Study the life of this person and see how he or she dealt with doubt.

3. Is there anyone in your life right now you need to *have mercy* on because he or she doubts? What could you do to encourage this person?

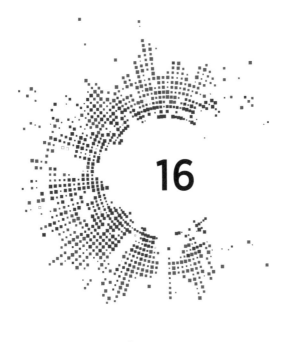

Legacy

What will they remember?

What you leave behind is not what is engraved in stone monuments but what is woven into the lives of others.
—Pericles

Mount Everest towers five-and-one-half miles above the face of the earth. It is a mystical mountain that has lured countless adventurers in attempts to scale its peak. George Mallory was once asked why he wanted to climb Mount Everest. His response was immediate and brief: "Because it is there!" Conquering mountains, literally or figuratively, has always been a challenge for humanity. Many years ago Edmund Hillary and Tenzing Norgay, his guide, led the first successful assault on Mount Everest. Week after week they inched up the world's tallest mountain. Herculean odds opposed them. Avalanches threatened to claim their lives. As they ascended the mountain the wind blew harder, the obstacles were greater, and the air became thinner. As they built new camps, their group became smaller and smaller as more and more of the expedition team retreated. Finally, at 11:45 a.m. on May 29, 1953, Edmund Hillary and Tenzing Norgay stood on top of the world. In his autobiography Hillary describes the exhilaration of becoming the first to stand on top of Mount Everest. But to me the most incredible thing is how brief their moment lasted. Fifteen minutes and then they were forced to begin their descent. If they had stayed any longer, they would not have made it back to their base camp by nightfall and they would have perished in the elements. All of that effort and sacrifice for fifteen minutes on top of the world.

I thought about this story on a motorcycle ride to the highest point in Indiana. Hoosier Hill is the highest natural point in the state. An Eagle Scout candidate working with the property owner constructed a trail, sign, and picnic area at this spot, 1,257 feet above sea level. Midwesterners are not as familiar with mountains, but I think almost everyone has his or her own Mount Everest. Some goal to scale the upper heights, some ambition to make it to the top, some motive to walk among the great, to be *somebody,* to leave a legacy!

Moses started out his life thinking he was somebody. Moses, the prince of Egypt, growing up in the Pharaoh's palace, educated with the best the world had to offer, was convinced at the age of forty that he was somebody who could make a difference. I think you could say though that he had climbed the ladder only to discover that it was leaning up against the wrong mountain. In less than fifteen minutes Moses had killed a man and in less than fifteen minutes he discovered that people knew what he had done—so he fled Egypt for the desert. In the desert he learned a lot about himself, a lot about God, and I think a lot about mountains.

In my own life I have discovered that **God always uses deserts to teach us dependence and mountains to give us perspective.** Moses gained some perspective on a mountain.

> *Then Moses climbed Mount Nebo*
> *from the plains of Moab to the top of Pisgah,*
> *across from Jericho. There the Lord*
> *showed him the whole land.*
> *(Deuteronomy 34:1)*

I don't know about you, but I wonder what Moses must have thought as he stood on top of Mount Nebo and looked at where they had come from and where they were going and realized that he was not going to actually take possession of the promised land. He had climbed his last mountain, but the significance was this: Moses climbed all his mountains with God.

The goal of the Christian life is to ascend the holy hill. We do that when we surrender our self-will of ambition, which strives for human achievement at the expense of knowing God personally. It is the essence of living last. The surrendered spirit wants the holy hill. Moses knew about surrender. The psalmist asked the question in Psalm 24:3—"Who may ascend the mountain of the Lord? Who may stand in his holy place?" Moses could have answered this question, because after a lot of trying and failing he got it right. The only ones who can climb the holy hill are those who are seeking God.

Deuteronomy 34 is the last written chapter in the life of Moses, but his life would live on because he would leave a legacy. We are in the process of leaving a legacy, and we are recipients of what those who have come before us have left for us. Those who come behind us will receive what we pass on to them. As individuals we are leaving legacies and I think it wise to stop and think occasionally about what we are leaving for future generations, asking the question, "What will we be remembered for?"

A couple of chapters back I gave some examples of some unique tombstone messages. Though we don't see this much anymore, for many years epitaphs gave us some insight into what people chose to remember about their loved ones or in some cases their not-so-loved ones. A friend sent me a copy of some actual inscriptions on tombstones:

> In East Dalhousie Cemetery, Nova Scotia:
> *Here lies Ezeakial Aikle, Age 102, The Good Die Young.*

> In a London cemetery:
> *Here lies Ann Mann, Who lived an old maid but died an old Mann, Dec. 8, 1767.*

> In Ribbesford, England, cemetery:
> *Anna Wallace, the Children of Israel wanted bread and the Lord sent them manna. Old clerk Wallace wanted a wife, and the Devil sent him Anna.*

Uniontown, Pennsylvania:
*Here lies the body of Jonathan Blake, stepped on
the gas instead of the brake.*

Silver City, Nevada:
*Here lays Butch; we planted him raw. He was quick
on the trigger but slow on the draw.*

Boot Hill Cemetery in Tombstone, Arizona:
*Here lies Lester Moore. Four slugs from a .44.
No less, no more.*

Nantucket, Massachusetts:
*Under the sod and under the trees lies the body of
Jonathan Pease. He is not here; there's only the pod:
Pease shelled out and went to God.*

Albany, New York:
*Harry Edsel Smith, Born 1903. Died 1942. Looked
up the elevator shaft to see if the car was on the
way down. It was.*

On a more serious note, if you were to write your own epitaph, what might it be? Put the book down for a minute, grab a pen, and think about what you think people will remember about your life. Kind of tough, isn't it? Every day we add to our legacy when we answer that question. You may never climb Mount Everest or even Mount Nebo, but you are given the opportunity to climb the holy hill of surrender and you do not have to travel to some far-off place to climb that hill. Moses was a Live*Last* kind of guy and his example in this last chapter of Deuteronomy gives us some questions that might help us consider our legacy.

Question One:
Whom did you really love?

"Since then, no prophet has risen in Israel like Moses, whom the Lord knew face to face" (Deuteronomy 34:10).

If you have any questions at all about whom or what you love, ask your family. They can tell you. You cannot hide love. It shows up in all kinds of places—obvious places like your face and the tone of your voice, other places like your calendar and even in some not-so-obvious places like your checkbook. Whom or what you love is not hard to figure out. Your family knows, your friends know, your neighbors and coworkers might even know. We have a hard time hiding whom or what we love.

Study the life of Moses and you will come away knowing that Moses loved God with all his heart, soul, mind, and strength, and he loved his people. On a pretty regular basis, the children of Israel were selfish, stubborn, and sinful. But Moses was their leader and he loved them in spite of it all. And more than that, he loved God, and they knew it.

Let me ask you a very pointed and personal question: Does your family know that you know and love God?

Now the question is not "Does your family know you know *about* God?" I believe it's very possible to know about God but not really know and love God.

When your life is over, you cannot add to your legacy. Your legacy is left behind. I believe there is nothing more important for you to leave behind than the knowledge that you loved God with all your heart, soul, mind, and strength.

The children of Israel had no doubt about the love that Moses had for God. Moses had a relationship with God that was unlike that of anyone else. It is a relationship that had been known only by Adam and Eve in the Garden of Eden before the fall. One of the items the children of Israel would not soon forget was the tent that Moses used to pitch outside the camp. He called it the Tent of Meeting. Anyone who wanted to pray could go out to this Tent of Meeting. When Moses would go to the tent, all the people would stand at the entrances to their tents and watch what would happen. The pillar of cloud would come down and stay at the entrance to this Tent of Meeting while the Lord spoke with Moses. Exodus tells us that the people would all stand and worship while Moses was in the Tent of Meeting.

The Lord would speak to
Moses face to face,
as one speaks to a friend.
(Exodus 33:11)

Numbers tells a story of when Miriam and Aaron opposed Moses. *Moses was a very humble man, more humble than anyone else on the face of the earth* (Numbers 12:3). When brother and sister ganged up on him, God called a meeting in the Tent of Meeting, and the Bible is quite clear that God was very unhappy with Aaron and Miriam. This is what God said to them:

When there is a prophet among you,
I, the Lord, reveal myself to them in visions,
I speak to them in dreams.
But this is not true of my servant Moses;

he is faithful in all my house.
With him I speak face to face,
clearly and not in riddles;
he sees the form of the Lord.

(Numbers 12:6–8)

The point is simply this: God loved Moses. Moses loved God. And when Moses was gone, there was never a doubt about their relationship. They remembered who Moses loved.

Question Two:
What did you do for the kingdom?

If conversations at your house are anything like mine, you probably find yourself answering a question about your day's activities. Can you imagine how Moses might have answered the question "Did you do anything today?"

Depending on what day it was, he would have had quite a story. There was the parting of the Red Sea, there was the day when God had him throw the piece of wood into the waste water and it became sweet, or how about the first time Moses gave them instructions about manna and quail from heaven? There was the day that he struck the rock with his staff and water flowed from it, or how about the day when Aaron and Hur helped him hold his hands up all day so the Israelites could defeat the Amalekites? Maybe the most significant day was when Moses went mountain climbing and while Israel was camped in the desert, he met with God. On Mount Sinai God made a covenant with Moses and the children of Israel and gave him the Ten Commandments. When the children of Israel remembered what Moses had done for the kingdom, this is what they said:

> Who did all those miraculous signs and
> wonders the Lord sent him to do in Egypt. . . .
> For no one has ever shown the mighty power or
> performed the awesome deeds that
> Moses did in the sight of all Israel.
> (Deuteronomy 34:11–12)

He had some big days of kingdom work, but the bottom line is that Moses was obedient, and that's all God asks from you or me. I know you know this, but it bears repeating: only what is done for the kingdom will last. Everything else passes away. Jesus would come and speak these words from another mountain:

> "Do not store up for yourselves
> treasures on earth, where moth and
> rust destroy and where thieves break in and steal."
> (Matthew 6:19 ESV)

Here's another very personal question: What are you doing for the kingdom? What continuing contribution are you making to build the kingdom? Most of us will never have opportunities to do those giant things as Moses did, but we can contribute to the kingdom every single day. Many, maybe most, of those contributions are offered without ever leaving our homes. We make them as we love our families and raise up our children to love and honor God. We make them in our offices as we are people of honesty and integrity in the midst of a society that thinks character doesn't count. I promise you that when your legacy is examined, what you did to build the kingdom will be remembered.

Question Three:
How did you handle disappointment?

For me this may be the toughest legacy question, but it is so very important for us to consider. You may not agree, but I believe we are all remembered for how we handle disappointment. Into every life disappointment will come, things will not go our way, and life will not be fair. And you can count on one more thing too: people will be watching. When there's a big game on television, millions of people will be watching, and when the game is over they always want to interview the winners. And generally they make idiots out of themselves. Maybe I'm the only one, but I'm always anxious to see how people handle losing.

Moses had some tremendous disappointments in his life, but Deuteronomy 34 has to reveal the biggest one:

> *Then the Lord said to him, "This is the land*
> *I promised on oath to Abraham, Isaac and Jacob when*
> *I said, 'I will give it to your descendants.' I have let you*
> *see it with your eyes, but you will not cross over into it."*
> *(Deuteronomy 34:4)*

I read that verse and I find myself saying, "That's not fair! No one deserved to go into the promised land more than Moses." He had put up with the whining and complaining. He had watched them pick up rocks in anger ready to stone him. He had changed their diapers and given them pacifiers time and time again. Moses had even gone to God and begged for the forgiveness of the children of Israel in their rebellion. I understand why God would not let that generation go into the promised land, but it just doesn't seem fair that Moses had to suffer with them. Joshua and Caleb got to go—it seems that Moses should have too. When he stood on top of Mount Nebo, he was not hearing for the first time that he would not enter into the promised land. He had lived with that disappointment for a long time. But his disappointment with circumstances did not keep him from loving God, and it did not keep him from being obedient in kingdom work. You see, Moses knew that people were watching.

By now you know another personal question is coming: How do you handle disappointment? I hope and pray that your family, friends, and coworkers will see how you respond not only to winning but also to losing.

Question Four:
Who followed in your footsteps?

Most kids I know like to play this game with their moms or dads. It was one of my kids' favorites. They would stand on my feet and I would walk—or at least attempt to. This game doesn't last too many years, of course—the kids get too heavy and their feet too big.

While that's just a game, what happens in the years to come is not. Our children in many ways will follow in our footsteps. They're a significant part of our legacy. We're modeling for them what really matters. Does that scare you? I don't think it should make us afraid, but I do think it should keep us on our knees.

We have the opportunity not just to mentor our children, but I believe God provides us with many more opportunities to mentor those coming down the road behind us. Moses had one following in his footsteps. His name was Joshua. Scripture tells us about their relationship:

> *Now Joshua son of Nun was filled*
> *with the spirit of wisdom because*
> *Moses had laid his hands on him.*
> *(Deuteronomy 34:9)*

Numbers 27 tells us the rest of the story.

> *So the Lord said to Moses, "Take Joshua son of Nun,*
> *a man in whom is the spirit of leadership, and lay*
> *your hand on him. Have him stand before Eleazar the*
> *priest and the entire assembly and commission him*
> *in their presence. Give him some of your authority so the*
> *whole Israelite community will obey him. He is to stand before*
> *Eleazar the priest, who will obtain decisions for him by*
> *inquiring of the Urim before the Lord. At his command*
> *he and the entire community of the Israelites will go out,*
> *and at his command they will come in." Moses did as*
> *the Lord commanded him. He took Joshua and had him*
> *stand before Eleazar the priest and the whole assembly. Then he*
> *laid his hands on him and commissioned him,*
> *as the Lord instructed through Moses.*
> *(Numbers 27:18–23)*

Can you imagine how hard that would have been? Moses was being replaced. The younger generation was assuming leadership. But he did not get jealous, he did not pout, he did not try to pick his own successor. He did exactly what God instructed him to do. And if you read on in the book of Joshua you'll discover that the godly influence of Moses continued through the life of Joshua.

My mentor was a successful pastor and denominational leader who saw something in me and believed in me and did everything he could to prepare me and encourage me, including giving me some of his authority. When I think of him—and I think of him often—I think of a man who loves God and has invested his life in building the kingdom. I watched how he handled disappointment on more than one occasion, and I learned some powerful lessons. Today I'm following in his footsteps. I will always be grateful to him. As you consider your spiritual mentor, today would be a great day to pause and thank God for the one who has touched your life in that special way.

Here are some more personal and probing questions: Who are you mentoring spiritually? Are you living a holy life that's a model for those that are watching you? Are your habits and attitudes, words and actions such that they bring honor and glory to God? Are you taking time for the people who need you the most? Maybe, even in this moment, you would ask God to help you be a mentor who makes the difference in the lives of those following in your footsteps.

Question Five:
When did you stop growing?

I love this verse:

Moses was a hundred and
twenty years old when he died,
yet his eyes were not weak nor his strength gone.
(Deuteronomy 34:7)

God led Moses to climb Mount Nebo. He showed him the promised land. Moses died, and Scripture tells us that God made all the funeral arrangements—no farewells, no fanfare. He simply laid down and the Lord took his spirit. Moses died alone, without family or friends standing at his side. But Moses died secure, forever safe in the arms of a loving God. There were no solemn processions, no stately funeral. The Lord buried him privately. Moses had finished the race, he had kept the faith; God took him for his crown. "His eyes were not weak nor his strength gone." What an epitaph!

At the time of his death Moses was one hundred twenty years old. He had lived through twelve decades of hope and hardship—forty years as the prince of Egypt, forty years of obscurity in the desert, and forty years leading a caravan of grumblers through the desert. Through all this Moses never stopped growing.

The happiest, most fulfilled people I know are those who spend a lifetime growing in their love and knowledge of the Lord. And I'm convinced that those closest to us know when we quit growing.

It can happen to you. You've heard hundreds, maybe thousands of sermons and Sunday School lessons. Maybe you've even been the one to preach or teach them, and somewhere along the way you got lazy, or maybe proud, and you just quit growing. The people closest to you know it. I want to be a lifelong learner. I want God to be teaching me things as long as my eyes are not weak and my strength is not gone!

Years ago I wrote these words in my journal: "For most of us, our legacy will *not* be one big thing—a job, a decision, an event. But it consists of lots of little things—an act of kindness, consistency of service, an encouraging word, time invested."

Questions for Reflection

1. Who is your spiritual mentor? Have you said thanks to him or her?

2. What are the three most important lessons you've learned from your spiritual mentor?

3. Whom are you mentoring spiritually?

Conclusion

Who Do You Say Jesus Is?

Jesus Christ did not say, "Go into the world and tell the world
that it is quite right."
—C. S. Lewis

Human attention span has supposedly dropped from twelve seconds in 2002 to only eight seconds today, which is terribly frightening when you consider that the attention span of a goldfish is nine seconds. What do you say to folks like that?

Throughout this book we've started each chapter with a question, closed each chapter with some questions for reflection, and scattered a few questions in between. So here's one more: **What do you want next?**

While I don't love quizzes, I do love questions. Curious by nature, I love asking questions.

The words *quiz, quest,* and *question* come from the same root word in Latin that means "to seek, search, and ask," literally or figuratively. All through school we're asked questions. We're required to answer questions for a grade, and even when we graduate, life is filled with many more moments of asking and answering questions. Jesus seemed to love questions too. He asked quite a few of them—three hundred seven to be exact.

Jesus *was asked* one hundred eighty-three questions.
He answered only three.

Jesus operated His own little unaccredited university. He only had twelve full-time students, and one of them flunked out. It does not appear that He was very choosy about His students. There does not appear to have been any entry exams: no ACT, no SAT. Jesus operated His own honors college, Peter, James, and John being the members. There were extra-curricular activities—adventure learning seemed to be a major component—and it appears that their food service might have been inconsistent, but at times, spectacular. Their commencement exercise does not appear to have featured any diplomas, but they were commissioned—followed by the extraordinary sight of seeing Jesus ascend into the sky.

These graduates found themselves staring up into the sky asking the question, *What's next?*

In our culture we don't look to the sky. Instead, we look to what many have described as the number-one killer of productivity on the planet: the smart phone, something owned by seven out of ten Americans. For the children who have grown up with them—they provide not only a distraction but an addiction as well.

The disciples of Jesus didn't have Google or Siri for help with an answer. What did we do without Google and Siri?

For those of you who have been living on another planet or, like me, were born back when dinosaurs were walking the earth, Siri is a computer program that works an intelligent personal assistant or knowledge navigator. Can you believe that Siri was given an honorary degree in humanities at the University of Florida in spring 2015? Siri is smart and can answer lots and lots of questions for you or at least direct you to a place where you can find an answer.

Google is now more than two decades old. It was first registered as a domain in September 1997. The name "Google" is a play on the word *googol*, which is a mathematical term that represents the number one plus one hundred zeros, and "it reflects the founders' mission to organize a seemingly infinite amount of information on the web." Originally released in ten languages, today it is in more than one hundred fifty!

I'm a Google fan, but Google and Siri won't be of great help in answering the question "What do I want next?"

While it's true that Google and Siri could help you find your way to a destination, provide you with information about housing, restaurants, job opportunities, and maybe even the best place to purchase a ring; when it comes to those *big rock* questions in life, you need more than they can provide.

So I offer you six very quick thoughts as you finish this book (some of these are repeat messages from earlier,) and I promise that they will come in handy when life tests you—and trust me: life *will* test you!

1. Trust the compass, not the clock.

*"Seek first his kingdom and his righteousness,
and all these things will be given to you as well."*
(Matthew 6:33)

Fixing our eyes on Jesus, the pioneer and perfecter of faith.
(Hebrews 12:2)

Those are two of hundreds of verses that remind us about our priority—Jesus. We're living in a time that has so many options, and often the problem is that we want them all now. We're not very patient, and we have been programmed to be *instaholics*. We want what we want and we want it now. So here is my counsel and encouragement to you: trust the Creator, who knows you better than yourself, and not the calendar. Keep your eyes and your heart fixed on Jesus, and let Him take care of the timing. It has been my experience that impatience causes us to make really bad decisions. Trust God and His plan for all the details and all the days of your life.

2. Extend grace and stand for truth.

Why? The best reason is that when we do this, we are most like Jesus. In the gospel of John we are told that Jesus came from the Father "full of grace and truth" (John 1:15). Remember: we need both grace and truth and at the right time and in the right measures.

We live in a very conflicted world, and while it is not the only time in history when the United States has been so divided, social media seems to have raised the stakes. Not only can you see photos of what people are having for dinner or their favorite cat trick video—you can also read their opinion or perspective about virtually any subject.

Can I remind you that God chose for us to be living in this time and this space of history? We have an opportunity to engage with culture and make a difference in our corners of the world.

One of the challenges of the church today is to *extend grace and stand for truth.* We love sinners (or at least we say we do), and loving them represents grace. We hate sin, and that represents truth. Unfortunately, it's easy to confuse the two and end up hating sinners and loving sin. Grace demands that we work hard to understand the truth of Scripture so that we will not fall short of it because of emotional or cultural pressure—but also so we will not go beyond it and become stricter than God would be.

Extend grace and stand for truth, and remember—always lead with grace. Do that, and you are acting like Jesus!

3. Keep a great pit crew.

Sounds like an advertisement for NASCAR. I've never been to a NASCAR event (don't judge me). I've never watched more than about ten minutes of a NASCAR race, but my favorite part is watching the pit crew change tires, clean windshields, fill it up with gas, and seeing how quickly they can do that.

My advice is simply this: keep a great pit crew! You'll need them. As you make your way through life, stay connected with family, with a church, with a community who can help keep you accountable, and maybe help you change a tire (literally and metaphorically).

4. Soak in Scripture—daily.

If you want answers to all the questions you'll encounter in life, start every single day with time in God's Word. My prediction is that you'll have fewer questions, you'll experience less stress, and you'll be a "go to" person for others if you soak in Scripture. Read it, pray it, memorize it, sing it, share it, and depend upon it. If you want to know all the benefits of Scripture in your life, read Psalm 119 at least once a month.

Failing to spend time in God's Word is a bit like skipping the locker room on the way to play football, trying to ride a bicycle with two flat tires, or trying to quench your thirst with a carbonated drink. Life will be harder—trust me. Follow the counsel of the apostle Paul: "Put on the full armor of God" (Ephesians 6:11). If you don't believe me, do the research; conduct an experiment. Compare a week in the Word daily with a week away from the Word. Here's what I believe you'll find: you'll have problems and difficulties in both weeks—that's called life. But I'm confident that your week in the Word will be more peaceful and more powerful.

5. Pray big!

I have a sign in my office with these two words: *Pray big.* I have it there not for others but for me. I need to be reminded every day that I have a heavenly Father who does not restrict what I ask Him for. In fact, just the opposite—His Word encourages me to pray big because He wants to do exceedingly abundantly more than I can ask or imagine. So while you're soaking in His Word daily, pray big daily. Pray big for our world! Pray big for your family and friends! And oh, by the way, God's Word tells us to pray *continually*!

6. Never be afraid to ask questions.

I love people who ask questions because it tells me that they want to be lifelong learners, and if you're going to live last then you'll need to keep learning lessons along the way. Live*Lasters* are continuing to seek and striving to get better in their professions, as parents, as spouses, and as fully devoted followers of Jesus Christ.

Simon Peter, one of the inner-circle disciples of Jesus, asked lots and lots and lots of questions. Here's a quick sample:

- "Lord, how many times shall I forgive my brother or sister who sins against me?" (Matthew 18:21).

- "Lord, to whom shall we go?" (John 6:68).

- "Lord, are you going to wash my feet?" (John 13:6).

- "Lord, where are you going?" (John 13:36).

- "Lord, why can't I follow you now?" (John 13:37).

- "Lord, what about him?" (John 21:21).

Never be afraid to ask questions, but make certain you can answer this one:

> *Jesus: "Who do you say that I am?"*
> *(Luke 9:20 NASB)*

I'm from Texas, and there we would say that the granddaddy of all the three hundred seven questions asked by Jesus is this one. Google and Siri can't help with this question. It's enormous, ginormous, the biggest of all questions in my mind.

Jesus wanted to know His disciples' answer to this question, and I believe He wants to know ours as well. You could easily make a case that it's the most important question ever to be asked and answered. *Who do you say that I am?* Now Jesus knew who He was, of course, so He wasn't asking for His sake. He was asking for the disciples. Simon Peter, as he so often did, chose to speak up and answer the question:

> *"You are the Messiah sent from God!"*
> *(Luke 9:20 NLT)*

I'm not a prophet, but here's my prediction. Your life will be filled with many moments when you're faced with questions. There will be moments when you have far more questions than answers. Some of those questions will be beside a hospital bed, some by an open grave, and some on the side of a mountain.

In every situation I think the best way to respond is by hearing the voice of Jesus whisper these words: *Who do you say that I am?* And then you answer, **You are God's Messiah, my Savior, the anchor of my soul, my rock and my salvation, my refuge in times of trouble, my King, my Counselor, my Prince of Peace, my everlasting Father.**

I leave you a prayer offered by the late Brennan Manning. He shared this benediction at the close of a chapel service I was attending. I think about it often. He prayed—

> *May all your expectations be frustrated.*
> *May all your plans be thwarted.*
> *May all your desires be withered into nothingness—*
> *that you may experience the powerlessness and*
> *poverty of a child and sing, dance, and trust in the*
> *love of God, who is Father, Son, and Spirit. Amen.*

ABOUT the AUTHOR

DR. KEITH NEWMAN was elected as the fifteenth president of Southern Nazarene University in March 2017. With nine years of service as a Houston police officer, seventeen years of pastoral ministry in the Church of the Nazarene, and sixteen years as a senior administrator in Christian higher education, Dr. Newman counts it a great privilege to join a Christ-centered community preparing God-called, purpose-driven, passionate servant leaders who make the world better.

Keith loves to read stories, hear stories, and tell stories, and he believes God is in the middle of all our stories. Spending time with students is at the top of his list of favorite moments each week.

ABOUT
SOUTHERN NAZARENE UNIVERSITY

Founded in 1899, Southern Nazarene University is a private, Christian, liberal arts university—a service of the Church of the Nazarene. Located on a forty-acre campus just west of Oklahoma City, SNU grew out of several small colleges committed to educating people for lives of service to God, leadership, and reconciliation toward their neighbors and within the global community. More than 32,000 alumni work and serve throughout the United States and the world.